Un–Lease
Your Business

Un-Lease Your Business

How Smart Entrepreneurs Unlock Wealth, Autonomy and Control By Owning Their Building and Firing Their Landlord

Paul M. Neal

Vantage Point Commercial Capital, LLC
1545 Crossways Blvd.
Suite 250
Chesapeake, VA 23320, USA
Web: VPC.Capital

Ordering Information:
Quantity sales. Special discounts are available on quantity purchases by corporations, associations, and others. For details, contact the "Special Sales Department" at the address above.

Un-Lease Your Business, Paul M. Neal – 1st ed ISBN 978-1-955242-74-5

Table of Contents

Unlock Your Bonus Content NOW!

Reading 'Un-lease Your Business' is already a big step towards securing your future, but why stop there?

Accelerate your journey by accessing a suite of exclusive FREE resources, designed to deepen your understanding and fast-track your success. No need to wait until you've turned the last page - start enhancing your experience right away!

1. *The Ultimate Guide to Evaluating a Property:* Get your hands on our straightforward, step-by-step checklist to aid you in making an informed decision when eyeing that potential property. Understand the nuances of property evaluation, making it a smooth ride for you.

2. *Expert Insights: A Multi-Part Video Course:* Gain critical insights from seasoned professionals

who've walked the path you're about to tread. It's like having a panel of top-notch mentors right at your fingertips, helping you navigate your way to real estate wealth.

3. *Profitable Transitions: Real-World Case Studies of Entrepreneurs Turning Rent into Equity:* Hear directly from those who've done it. Their trials, tribulations, and triumphs - unfiltered, insightful, and most importantly, applicable to your own journey.

Visit the link or scan the QR code to access these powerful tools now. Remember, the road to business freedom and wealth creation begins with the first step.

www.OwnYourBuildingNow.com/Resources

OR

Introduction

Diving Into Wealth: The Real Estate Passport

"Real estate is an imperishable asset, ever increasing in value. It is the most solid security that human ingenuity has devised. It is the basis of all security and about the only indestructible security." - Russell Sage

Congratulations, entrepreneur! The fact that you're holding this book is a testament to your drive and ambition. You're likely a dynamic individual, someone who's carved out their corner in the local business landscape, running a thriving operation that's been growing for several years. Your enterprise is not a fledgling startup; it's a solidly established venture with a robust cash flow, supported by a team of anywhere between 5 to 20+ employees. You're making waves in your industry, and your presence is felt and respected.

This book is here to acknowledge your success, your dedication, and your commitment, but it also serves a grander purpose. It's not just a pat on the back; it's a tool, a guide, and a blueprint designed to propel you towards even greater success.

You see, you didn't simply enter the business world for the sake of it. No, you embarked on this journey driven by a vision of financial independence. You sought freedom and control, backed by an unyielding belief in your ability to outpace the competition. You were fueled by a dream of creating wealth and ensuring an excellent lifestyle for your family – a comfortable home, exciting opportunities to travel, and the means to leave a positive and lasting impact on your community.

As you navigate the landscape of business ownership, you've leaned on the expertise of professionals like CPAs and attorneys. You've recognized the value of their guidance in elevating your business to the next level. Similarly, this book is a professional service of sorts, dedicated to an aspect of your enterprise that has the potential to dramatically boost your financial independence: owning your commercial space.

This chapter is a celebration of your entrepreneurial spirit and an introduction to the journey you're about to embark on. It's a roadmap to transforming the dream of financial independence into your living reality. As you navigate this path, you're not just seeking immediate benefits for your business. You're laying the groundwork for long-lasting impacts on your wealth, your independence, and the legacy you'll leave behind.

Why Own the Real Estate Where Your Business Operates?

Achieving the heights of financial independence is not a simple feat. It's a multifaceted goal, intricate in its complexity and vast in its scope. There are multiple routes you can take, each with its unique challenges and rewards. However, for those of us who are entrepreneurs, one path shines more brightly than others. It's a journey that emboldens the entrepreneurial spirit and offers unprecedented opportunities to secure your financial future: owning the commercial space in which your business operates.

In business, real estate isn't just about physical space. It's more than four walls within which you conduct your operations. It's an asset, a tool, a stepping-stone on your pathway to the heights of financial independence. It represents an opportunity to consolidate your successes, magnify your profits, and fortify your business against the unexpected turns that inevitably come with the territory.

As the captain at the helm of your business, you navigate through uncertainty, embrace challenges, and champion adaptation. In this ever-evolving landscape, owning your commercial space equips you with a unique form of stability. It's an anchor amidst the tumultuous seas of market flux, providing you with a platform that remains steadfast through change.

But it's not just about stability. It's about taking your achievements thus far and catapulting them into a new realm of financial growth. With ownership comes the opportunity for appreciation, allowing your commercial space to not only serve as your business's home base but also as an asset that increases in value over time.

Moreover, it's about control. When you own your commercial space, you cease to be at the mercy of landlords, no longer needing to brace against rent hikes or the prospect of your lease not being renewed. It puts the power back in your hands, giving you greater control over your business's destiny.

Owning your space is a strategic move, one that calls upon your entrepreneurial acumen and taps into the core of why you ventured into business: to establish a durable legacy, to secure your financial independence, and to ensure that the fruits of your labor create a meaningful and lasting impact.

This goal of financial independence, though lofty, is far from unattainable. And as we delve deeper into the intricacies of owning your turf, you'll discover just how reachable it truly is.

There is No Straight Path to Success in Life

Navigating the path to ownership is an undertaking that requires strategic planning, careful consideration, and resilience. The process is fraught with potential stumbling blocks - from securing financing and finding the right location to negotiating terms and dealing with unforeseen issues that inevitably crop up. Moreover, there are inherent risks tied to owning real estate that, if not well managed, could deter your progress.

These obstacles may seem daunting and may even lead some entrepreneurs to question whether the rewards truly outweigh the challenges. But, rest assured, every entrepreneur who has achieved success has, at some point, faced their share of hurdles. The key is not to avoid these challenges, but to face them head-on, equipped with the right information and guidance.

The alternative, of course, is to continue leasing. But this path comes with its own set of risks and challenges. It leaves you at the mercy of your landlord, with no control over annual rent hikes or the eventual renewal of your lease.

You'll be investing hard-earned money into a property that you have no claim to, with every rental payment serving as a reminder of an opportunity missed.

And then there are the potential financial implications of not acting. The costs associated with leasing a commercial space can eat away at your profits over time, whereas owning your commercial space can provide potential financial benefits in the form of property appreciation and tax deductions. The longer you wait to make the leap, the greater the opportunity cost and the further away you may find yourself from your goal of financial independence.

Choosing not to act also means missing out on the power of leverage. The equity built up in your property can be utilized to fuel further growth, whether it's expanding your current business or branching out into other investment opportunities. It's an opportunity to build wealth and create an income stream outside of your primary business operations.

However, the most compelling argument for purchasing your own commercial space extends beyond the purely financial. It's about taking a significant step towards cementing your legacy, making a lasting mark, and having something tangible to show for your years of hard work and dedication. It's about taking control of your future and making a strategic decision that could propel your business and personal wealth to new heights. The path may be challenging, but the potential rewards are enormous.

What You'll Get From This Book

But alas! There is good news. It's where this book fits into your journey. Its purpose? To be your compass, your guide and trusted advisor, navigating you through the complexities and pitfalls associated with owning your commercial space. This book isn't a pitch, but a partner; your partner in taking an enormous leap towards your independence.

We stand together, you and I, on the cusp of an adventure. An adventure not marked by mythical beasts or hidden treasures, but by milestones of business achievements, fiscal responsibility, and the pursuit of a dream. This isn't just another journey - it's your journey towards a whole new level of success for you and your family.

Consider this book your GPS, your detailed map through the owner-occupied commercial real estate world. It isn't merely a collection of words and pages, but an actionable blueprint, a guide armed with practical steps, wisdom to shed light on unseen pitfalls, and strategies to avoid them. And when you stumble - as every entrepreneur does - this book will be there to help you get back on your feet, dust yourself off, and continue pressing forward.

But the book isn't just filled with advice - it's brimming with real-world stories of people like you, entrepreneurs who took the leap, who battled against the odds, who weathered the storm and emerged victorious. These are the stories of men and women who now stand proud, owning the space their businesses call home. They share their experiences, their wins and their losses, not to boast, but to inspire, to guide, and to assure you that the path is navigable.

So, as we begin this journey together, remember that this book is more than just a guide. It's an invitation to act, to step up, to break free from the shackles of uncertainty and embark on a path towards a brighter, secure future. Embrace it, for it is your first step into a process that could redefine your business and personal wealth.

Chapter 1

The Money Drain: Plugging the Monthly Leak

"The quickest way to double your money is to fold it over and put it back in your pocket." - Will Rogers

Navigating the changing sea of business ownership is no easy task. You're constantly confronted with shifting markets, evolving employee dynamics, and fluid organizational structures. Amid this constant flux, growth emerges as both a blessing and a challenge, often diverting hard-earned money down unseen drains.

One of the recurrent matters that you will face if you have a locally based business or a business that requires a physical location is the question: ***Do I rent or do I own that space?*** With a small, fragile, up and coming business, it is a simple answer. You rent. Your focus needs to be on building a solid, stable, growing enterprise that can fuel your life's dreams. But if you have been in business for a few years and have a successful growing track record, the answer is not as easy. While continuing to rent your space can be the default option, it may not be the best choice for your overall business success.

One of the most fundamental ideas you have to consider is why you went into business in the first place. For myself and many entrepreneurs, it was to achieve freedom and the wealth to enjoy it. To have the ability to call my own shots and to spend my time and my life with those people and doing the things that I wanted to do. And to achieve these goals sooner rather than later in life. But renting the space that my business operated out of did not fit into that wealth and freedom plan.

Number one, rent is a huge waste of money. It is typically the largest fixed overhead expense a business will incur... Every single month, paying the landlord - not yourself - thousands of dollars, which just feels bad. Sure, you get something valuable in return, but once the money is spent it's gone forever. And there's nothing left to show for it. So many business owners are looking for the best ways to invest their excess earnings while at the same time they are literally walking on a potential gold mine every day.

I mean, do you rent the house that you live in? Sure, maybe you did when you were just getting started in life, but the plan was to eventually own your own home, right?

Why? For many reasons. But one of the biggest reasons is the wealth creation opportunity real estate affords. Most successful people look to be owners, not renters, and accumulate more value over time. And the most savvy ones look to buy assets that create wealth passively - whether they are working or not - and history proves that passive income is a winner. Paying rent in any form is anathema to that idea. It's revolting to a wealth creator.

Robert Kyosaki wrote the seminal book on the subject, *Rich Dad, Poor Dad*[1], where he argues the case for asset accumulation as the goal for a secure and abundant future. When you have an asset that makes you money, you have separated your time involvement from your income creation. In effect, you are no longer trading hours for dollars like most people do.

You already understand this concept. You have employees. Why do you hire someone to do a job for you with *their time* to produce a result on your behalf? You pay them for their time, but you are receiving a multiple back in terms of income. Owning your space can give you options in this arena as well. In some cases, you can leverage extra commercial space that you own for rental income, empowering someone else to help pay your mortgage.

---

[1] Kiyosaki, Robert T. *Rich Dad Poor Dad*. Warner Books Ed, 2000

And so the longer your business rents its space, the more of your own and your potential tenants' dollars go to make someone else's financial future brighter and more secure. They're the ones taking the vacations with their family to St. John where they enjoy the beautiful, soft sand and pristine, crystal blue waters of the Caribbean… while you're paying rent to their building and putting passive income dollars in their pocket. Doesn't sound like a great idea to me.

What about taxes? As your business becomes more and more successful, the IRS becomes your fanboy. They love you and they want more and more of your hard earned cash, and it becomes increasingly difficult to benefit from tax breaks and deductions. Most of these are phased out as your income grows. So not only are you making your landlord rich, you are making the government rich too. Now, I believe everyone should pay taxes, but let's be real. The more you make, the more they take in a highly disproportionate way.

But what if you could start to play the game in a way that helps you minimize Uncle Sam's deep reach into your pocket? Do you think that taxes will magically go down sometime in the future for you? If so, you are in la la land. There is no politician alive today that will not sell your firstborn child (and second and third, et cetera…) to buy themselves votes and secure more power. Okay, maybe that's a little bit extreme…there may be one or two out there that would not, but even that might be a stretch.

See, you have to realize that as a small business owner, you are the engine and driver of economic growth and the primary source of tax dollars. Small business owners employ most of the non-government employees in this country today. Government does not create growth or tax dollars, instead they have to get it from you to spend (mostly waste). Here is how it works in the real world - you take all the risk, and if successful, the government wants its "reward", which is your money.

I mentioned before the idea of accumulating assets that generate income as a master key to wealth creation and true freedom in your life. By building a successful business with systems and employees, you have accomplished that in one area, and you are to be congratulated. But why not leverage that success to buy the building you are in and create a second asset? By not owning your space, you are not only wasting your rent dollars and foregoing the tax benefits, but you also lose the opportunity to build real estate equity. The equity gained can become a large part of your net worth over time, opening doors of opportunity that will inevitably come your way. You want to be in a position to take advantage of these, not pass on them simply because you have no option.

Someone once said that the only guarantees in life are death and taxes, but there is actually a third guarantee: inflation. I remember when I first started driving, gas was about a dollar a gallon - a bit hard to believe, right? But pick anything today and, over time, prices go up. I was buying a certain brand of treats for my golden retriever at the grocery store the other day with my wife. It's important to me that he has clean teeth, and clean breath for sure. Now my dog Galileo is just over three years old. And in that short timeframe, I noticed the *same* bag of dog treats, purchased at the same store, went from $12 a bag when we first bought them to just over $18 a bag. Now, I don't know what the government says about the official inflation rate, but that is about a 50% raise in cost according to my math with just one product.

So take just about anything and prices go up over time. What about rent? Up? This can work to your advantage if you are charging a tenant rent, but not so much if you are paying it. What else? How about the cost of real estate? Yes, that is right. It goes up over time. Now some markets can be cyclical, but even in those markets over the long run, they tend to appreciate. By not owning your space today, it gets more and more expensive every year. Again, this is great news if you are the owner, but not so much if you are watching the owner get rich - and on *your* dollars and your sweat equity. And that means you must work harder or longer or both to achieve your financial goals and achieve your dreams for yourself and your family.

Chapter 2

Growth's Bumps and Triumphs

"Every problem is a gift—without problems we would not grow." - Tony Robbins

Now that you have a successful growing business, you may be facing additional challenges with your space. The first and most fundamental issue is this: Do you have the physical room to grow any larger? I had that issue at one point in one of my businesses. I needed to hire more team members to expand, but did not really have anywhere to put them. So, being very creative, I remember stuffing three new employees into a small, converted conference room made to fit only one table. And later putting cubicle dividers into a spare room that would normally fit at most two employees and making it work for six. Let's just say that they got to know each other very well, which did produce a side "benefit" of the arrangement. I got to referee and be involved in much more office "drama" than most likely would have occurred with a little breathing room.

Clearly, we were busting out at the seams and needed more room. I could not physically add another team member unless we moved or opened another location. And running two locations in the same geographic area we served meant two times the overhead and was overly complicated. Not to mention that managing teams at two locations can be difficult.

I have learned after owning six businesses that simplicity beats complexity in almost every case, but you *do* have to do something to make it work. Employees, especially the newer generations, expect and even demand "a good working environment" - to possibly include catered sushi on Wednesdays and vanilla lattes on Friday mornings. While these may or may not be part of your retention plan, the basics like room to operate and work efficiently and effectively are minimum basic requirements.

The Efficiency Trap: Is Your Business Falling Behind Without You Noticing?

On top of just the sheer space needed for a growing company, you need to think about how efficiently you are actually using your current space. As businesses evolve over time, and especially with faster growing companies, needs change and the way you operate also needs to change and improve to match. Your systems, both codified and followed, and the unwritten cultural systems that can end up ruling the day, should be re-evaluated from time to time, particularly as you begin to sense the need for more space.

There are entire schools of teaching on the idea of making your space and processes more efficient. Lean methodologies is one that comes to mind. With its roots in the manufacturing space dating back to the early days at Toyota, its popularity has grown as companies around the world began to see the benefits of this approach. Books like *The Machine That Changed the World*[2] by Womack, et al further popularized the concept, detailing the superiority of lean production over traditional mass production. Lean methodologies have been adopted across various industries beyond manufacturing, including services, healthcare, and software development. They have proven their universal applicability in improving process efficiency and reducing waste.

A good friend of mine and successful commercial builder, Steve, recently took ownership of a local cabinet company. Although the cabinet company was successful in its own right and had a proven track record, Steve noticed that they were doing things *the way they have always been done*[3], and had cobbled together processes

---

[2] Womack, James P., Daniel T. Jones, and Daniel Roos. *The Machine That Changed the World.* Rawson Associates, 1990

[3] Sometimes progress is good!

that did not make sense in this day and age. He noticed that they were wasting a lot of time, and it was chiefly due to the physical and organizational layout of the building.

Ever the successful entrepreneur and also a commercial builder, Steve recognized an opportunity for improvement, and he decided to "clean sheet" the layout (much to the chagrin of the team he inherited) and gut and renovate the space. At the same time, he was able to install a new, highly efficient cabinet machine. When his re-imagining of the space and processes was complete, his newly invigorated team was producing almost *two times the output* with the same work hours and staff size. How could you impact your profitability with a better space arrangement? What if you could build something just for your business that really worked?

Bound By Your Lease: When Landlords Hold The Power

In addition to growth limitations and lack of flexibility, what about control? As a successful business owner, you like to be in control. But when your business rents its space, there are definitive limits to that.

Landlords, the owners of the space, also like to exercise control. You're borrowing their asset for a time and as long as your needs align with theirs - all is well. But that can change, and often does over time.

Back to the idea of the renovation that Steve did so successfully - he was able to do that because he not only owned the business, but he also owned the building itself. He only had to visit his mirror to ask permission. Most landlords are not too keen on complete space renovations. They cost a lot of money...they can be disruptive to other tenants...and possibly damaging to the premises. And if you are fortunate enough to have a landlord that is open to the idea, it will always come at a cost. Either you will sink your own money into improving someone else's space (think chapter one, wasting thousands of dollars on rent...) or they will sometimes finance it for you. Many times that comes in the form of a new long-term lease extension where they bake in the costs. Either way, you are paying the freight and if you let them extend out your lease, then you stand to potentially face the growth challenges already mentioned.

There are other ways I see renters lose control with landlords. Lease non-renewals is one. There is no guarantee that when your lease comes up for renewal, the landlord will automatically extend again. If it suits their needs and their best interests, they will generally do it. If not, well then too bad, so sad! Then what do you do?

Or perhaps they choose to renew your lease, but the renewal rent rate is substantially higher than when you took possession of the space in the first place. How could that impact your bottom line?

In many cases, landlords know that they have you over a barrel since moving your enterprise, particularly at the last minute, can prove disruptive. What if your business needs to be in a particular area and your clients, customers, or patients will go somewhere else if you are not convenient anymore? Out of sight is also out of mind.

One of my clients, Osman, who owns several pizza restaurants, recently faced a similar challenge. A successful immigrant from Turkey, Osman had invested the last 10 years of his life building two successful locally-operated pizza restaurants, among other enterprises. One day, the landlord of one of his two locations decided to sell the building he was in, leaving Osman in a very difficult place.

His clientele was mostly local and he knew if he could not find a suitable replacement location very close to his existing establishment, he would lose a good percentage of his business. And he would have to find that alternative location quickly, as time was not on his side. He had invested over $80,000 renovating the kitchen and making it work efficiently for his processes and operation. And that meant that 10 years of blood, sweat and tears, building and serving the local customer base, all that equity and hard work could be literally thrown away.

The decision became very simple - buy the building himself or risk the loss of much of what he had built up to this point. Fortunately, I was able to help him buy the building with no disruption at all to his restaurant operations. Thankfully the landlord gave him the first right of refusal on the purchase, but if he had not, it would have been very ugly indeed for Osman as the alternative was not good.

So keep in mind, as you consider renting or buying your own space, that you have to make your moves before you run out of time. Many people want to wait for all conditions to be right, but the reality is, there will never be a perfect time. Perfect timing for anything in life is much more of an exception than a rule. Life and the world just does not operate that way. If you don't make an intentional decision to ride the horse of life, you will at some point be trampled on by that same horse. Choice and free will is one of the greatest gifts that our Creator gave us, not victimhood.

Chapter 3

Own Your Stage: Why Building Ownership Rocks

"Buying real estate is not only the best way, the quickest way, the safest way, but the only way to become wealthy." - Marshall Field

If you have a successful business with several years' positive growth and track record, a local presence requirement for employees and/or customers, and you intend to be in business for years to come, you *must* consider owning the space your business operates out of. It solves so many of the problems that I've already outlined.

It positions you for tremendous benefits in the future, such as the ability to build wealth faster, gain freedom and control over your operational destiny, and stick it (at least some of it, and legally...) to the tax man.

If you have built a growing, prosperous business, then you are *not* a renter in life, but an owner. Someone who likes to call their own shots and take the calculated risks that are always involved with stepping out into new territory. And you understand that there is no gain without stretching and expanding your vision and taking definitive action.

You are either growing and becoming more in life, or you are decaying. There is no coasting. So let's dive into some of the reasons *why* buying your building is a great business and wealth strategy for you.. But first, a few stories.

John's HVAC Company Story: How Owning His Space Transformed His Business

John, a good friend of mine, had spent the past five years building his HVAC company from the ground up. Through sheer determination and a commitment to excellent service, John's business had grown into one of the most successful HVAC companies in the region.

Despite his success, John couldn't help but feel the weight of the $6,200 per month rent he paid for his company's office and workshop space. As his business continued to grow, John knew he needed a larger facility to accommodate his expanding team and equipment. He also couldn't shake the feeling that he was throwing money away each month, making his landlord rich while gaining no equity for himself.

One day, while attending a local business networking event, John struck up a conversation with a fellow entrepreneur and client of mine who shared the story of how he had recently purchased a commercial property for his own business. Intrigued, John decided it was time to seriously explore the possibility of owning his own space.

Over the next few months, John researched the commercial property market and consulted with real estate experts. He discovered that by investing in a commercial property, he could not only provide his growing business with the space it needed but also build equity, generate income, and ultimately save money on his monthly expenses.

John began the search for the perfect property, and after several weeks of diligent searching, he found a building that was one and a half times the size of his current rented space. With the guidance of his real estate agent and our team, John secured the necessary financing and purchased the property.

With the new, larger building, John was able to comfortably accommodate his expanding team and equipment. But he didn't stop there. Recognizing the opportunity to generate additional income, John decided to rent out a portion of the unused space to other local businesses. To his delight, the rental income he received from his tenants was significant enough to cover a large part of his mortgage payment. In fact, his net monthly mortgage payment was even lower than the rent he had been paying for his previous, smaller space.

Now, when John looks back on the journey that led him to own his commercial space, he's filled with gratitude for the opportunities it has afforded him. No longer burdened by high and wasteful rent payments, John can focus on growing his business and providing for his family. Through determination, smart decision-making, and a willingness to seize the wealth opportunity under his feet, John turned his once-small HVAC business into a thriving enterprise with a bright future ahead.

A Veterinarian's Journey to Modernize Her Business and Position for the Future

Let me tell you about another inspiring story of commercial property ownership. It is about a veterinarian named Sarah who owns a thriving veterinary practice in a rapidly growing suburban community in Northern Virginia. As her business expanded, she found herself outgrowing her current leased space, which was not only too small, but also lacked the modern facilities her practice needed.

Sarah knew she had to make a change, but she was hesitant to sign another long-term lease that would tie her down and limit her ability to control the destiny of her business. After talking to other business owners in her area, she decided to explore the possibility of building a custom-tailored property for her veterinary practice.

With the help of a commercial real estate agent, Sarah found a piece of land in the perfect location that offered ample space for her practice and even had room for expansion. She purchased the property, and with the help of a talented architect, transformed it into a state-of-the-art veterinary facility.

By owning her building, Sarah not only eliminated the stress of rising rent prices and lease negotiations but also gained valuable equity in her property as it appreciated over time. The decision to buy her building allowed her to focus on providing the best care possible for her clients' beloved pets while also securing her financial future.

Do Not Miss Your Chance

Owning the commercial property where your business operates can be a powerful wealth-building strategy. You can create a stable foundation for your business, build equity, and potentially generate additional income by renting out unused space to other businesses.

As seen in the stories of John and Sarah, the journey to commercial property ownership can be filled with challenges and uncertainties, but the rewards can be immense. Both of them took calculated risks, and their hard work and determination paid off in the long run.

If you're a business owner who is tired of being a renter and wants to take control of your future, it's time to seriously consider the benefits of owning your building. Remember, you're an owner in life, not a renter. Embrace the challenge and seize the opportunities that lie ahead.

In the next chapter, let's take a deeper dive into some of the specific benefits and reasons for ownership.

Chapter 4

Tread on Treasure:
Your Land, Your Goldmine

"Landlords grow rich in their sleep without working, risking or economizing."
- John Stuart Mill

You should now start to get a sense that you can gain some significant wins if you buy your business's commercial space. In fact, it's the property right under your feet that could be the catalyst to accelerate your wealth accumulation. In this chapter, we'll take a closer look at multiple wealth-enhancing benefits and more. But before that, let's consider a few questions:

Why is it a good idea to start where you are? Simply put, it's just easier than searching outwardly for opportunity. As a business owner, you're already putting in the time, effort, and resources to grow your business and create a better future for yourself and those who depend on you. By looking under your feet and considering the ownership potential, you're laying the groundwork for a more prosperous and financially secure future. Plus, you're already busy running your business, so it makes sense to build on that investment by owning the space that it operates in.

Do you like wasting rent dollars and making someone else rich? Nobody likes to feel like they're just tossing their hard-earned money out the window, right? When you rent a commercial space, you're essentially paying someone else's mortgage and contributing to their wealth. By owning your property, you're investing in your own financial success, ensuring that the money you spend on your business space directly benefits you. Owning your operational space means you're putting that money back into your own pocket, building equity, and securing long-term financial stability. It means that every penny you spend on it is an investment in yourself and your future. Plus, it shows that you're serious about your business's growth and success. Now, doesn't that sound like a much better plan?

Laying the Foundation: How Building Equity Enhances Your Financial Portfolio

Being an owner means time is passively working for you, not against you, and you will be building equity in a real tangible asset. What's equity? It's the difference between your property's current market value and the outstanding balance on your mortgage. As you pay down your mortgage and your property's value increases, so does your equity. Building equity is a powerful way to create wealth and secure your financial future. Here's a deeper look at some ways it can positively impact your financial success:

1. **You are paying yourself first:** Owning your property ensures the money you spend on your business space directly benefits you. Instead of paying someone else's mortgage, you're investing in your own financial success.

2. **You can leverage that equity for future opportunities**: As your equity grows, you can use it as collateral to secure financing for other business ventures, property investments, or personal financial goals. This enables you to capitalize on new opportunities and expand your wealth.

3. **You are moving from a short-term to a long-term mindset:** Owning your space shifts your focus from short-term savings to long-term financial growth, building wealth, and securing your financial future.

4. **You are creating a systematic and forced savings plan:** Making regular mortgage payments on your commercial property acts as a form of forced savings, contributing to your

equity and bringing you closer to owning the property outright.

The Income Multiplier: Boosting Your Earnings

Generating additional income through commercial property ownership is another tremendous opportunity to substantially increase your long-term wealth and financial security. Let's explore some ways in which owning your space can help you generate additional income:

1. **You can rent out unused space:** Generate passive income by renting out extra space to other businesses. This also helps you establish connections with other local entrepreneurs, fostering a sense of community and collaboration.

2. **You can create advertising space:** Lease advertising space such as billboards, signage, or even cell phone antennas to other businesses or use it to promote your own products and services, creating another source of income.

3. **You can diversify your income streams:** Explore and house new businesses that complement your primary business, increasing your revenue and protecting your business from market fluctuations.

4. **You can realize increased property value:** As your commercial property's value increases over time, so does the potential for higher rental rates or a more valuable asset when you decide to sell, resulting in increased income.

5. **You are turning one profitable business into two:** Purchasing a commercial property effectively creates a second business – the real estate business. Building wealth through two interconnected ventures maximizes your financial potential.

The Value Play: Make Your Business Worth More

Owning your commercial space not only can grow your equity and generate additional income but also can increase the overall value of your business. Here are a few ways:

1. **You are enhancing its stability and financial strength:** Owning your property showcases your business's stability and financial strength, making it more attractive to potential investors, partners, and customers.

2. **You have a demonstrated long-term commitment to growth:** Investing in commercial property signals a long-term

commitment to growing and expanding your business, enhancing your company's reputation and attracting new clients.

3. **You can experience asset appreciation:** As your commercial property appreciates in value, so does the overall value of your business, which can be leveraged to secure financing for future growth opportunities or improve your business's financial standing.

4. **Your business is customizable and adaptable:** Owning your commercial space allows you to customize the property to suit your business's unique needs and requirements, increasing efficiency, improving customer satisfaction, and ultimately boosting your business's value.

5. **You are creating future opportunities:** Increased business value can lead to new opportunities, such as attracting investors, securing strategic partnerships, or expanding your operations, further contributing to the growth and success of your business.

Now that you have a solid understanding of the wealth-building opportunities that owning your commercial space can offer, let's take a look at another story which illustrates some of these key advantages.

Kathy is a successful doctor who, 15 years ago, made the wise decision to purchase the building where her thriving OB-GYN practice was located. Over the years, Kathy's practice grew and flourished, establishing her as a prominent local medical provider.

Fast forward to today, and Kathy's building is now paid off. Her business essentially rents the space from her, creating a unique situation where she benefits from both her practice income and the property ownership. Recently, her practice caught the attention of a larger medical group, which specializes in acquiring independent practices and integrating them into their organization.

Recognizing the value of Kathy's thriving local practice and the facility it operated from, the larger medical group not only acquired her practice, but also retained her as a key team member. This arrangement allowed Kathy to continue working in her practice for several more years, on her own terms.

Moreover, the larger medical entity agreed to pay rent for the building Kathy owned, effectively providing her with a substantial steady stream of retirement income for as long as she chooses to keep the property.

Kathy's story is a testament to the power of property ownership, showcasing how it can not only support a successful business but also provide financial security and retirement income. By investing in her building, Kathy not only secured her practice's future but also ensured her own financial well-being, ultimately leading to a highly rewarding outcome.

As we transition to the next chapter, we'll focus on another crucial aspect of long-term success – seizing control over your destiny. When you own your commercial space, you are less vulnerable to external factors such as rent increases, lease cancellations, or limitations on expansion.

Chapter 5

Steer Your Story: No More Playing the Victim

"You are always free to change your mind and choose a different future, or a different past." - Richard Bach

Let me tell you a little story about my friend Maria who had an amazing bakery in a rented space in Tulsa, OK. She spent years building a loyal customer base and was well-loved in the community. At lease renewal time, her landlord unexpectedly raised her rent significantly - citing inflation and his missed market opportunities with potential new renters as his primary motivations and drivers.

Being already tight on cash flow, Maria couldn't afford the substantial increase without making other changes in her operations, but felt like she had no other good options to keep her business on track. She was reaching the local community and was realizing her lifelong dream to bring joy and uplift people with her baking, and she was growing at a decent clip.

But the rent increase forced her to make a hard choice: cut staff and limit her growth or take a major pay cut herself until she could grow out of the problem. Ever the entrepreneur, she chose delayed gratification for herself - again. But there was another option available that she didn't know about…

The same goes for the risk you face of your space being sold to another owner. Imagine investing time, money, and effort into creating the perfect space for your business, only to be forced to move because the building was sold and the new owners aren't interested in your business.

I can't tell you how many opportunities we have had to help business owners buy their space when the landlord decides to sell unexpectedly. The p roblem w ith w aiting for this to occur is that it's a very reactive position to be forced into, and sometimes it works out, and other times it does not.

When you own proactively and by design, you're in control of your business's destiny. You can make decisions based on what's best for you and your company, not what's best for your landlord.

Moreover, owning your space allows you to build a stronger relationship with your community and establish a sense of permanence for your business. This stability can contribute to a positive reputation and help build trust with your clients, as they know you are committed to the area and invested in the long-term success of your business. This sense of permanence can also have a positive impact on your employees, providing them with a deeper feeling of job security and a stable work environment.

Gain More Decision–Making Power

Owning your space means you can make decisions that best serve your business. Flexibility is essential in today's fast-paced world, and having control over your space allows you to adapt as needed.

Consider the story of John who ran his digital marketing agency out of a rented office. As his business grew, John realized that reorganizing his office space could improve workflow efficiency. However, his landlord refused any significant changes. John had to work with what he had, leading to wasted space and cramped quarters. His employees were constantly bumping into each other, leading to frustration and inefficiencies. If John had owned his space, he could have made the necessary changes to boost productivity and keep his team happy.

Location is also crucial for success. Many businesses begin their life in an area that may not be optimal for their ultimate success, but serve as a good starting point. This is generally due to a number of factors, such as limited vision and experience, and budgetary constraints. Now that you have more of a track record and "next-level" thinking, you can strategically position your business to increase growth and revenue. You can also build to suit or renovate as needed, creating an environment that works specifically for your business.

Furthermore, as we've discussed, owning your commercial space allows you to diversify your income streams by potentially leasing out unused space to other businesses. This added revenue can offset your mortgage payments, reduce your overall operating costs, and contribute to your financial stability.

Creating a "Wow" Experience Can Be Your Game Changer

Everyone knows today that the customer experience is king. Great experience equals great reviews equals more referrals and business growth. It is the cheapest form of advertising you can do. Owning your operational space opens up endless possibilities for creating an unforgettable customer and employee experience.

You can design the domain to reflect your business's values, cater to your customers' specific needs, and create a work environment that your employees love.

Think about it: when customers walk into your business, they should be wowed by the atmosphere and overall positive feeling. That's where the magic happens! When you own your space, you can customize every aspect to leave a lasting impression on your customers, encouraging repeat visits and brand loyalty. From creating welcoming waiting areas to incorporating comfortable seating, a personalized space goes a long way in enhancing the customer experience.

Let's not forget about your employees. You can create a work setting that attracts and retains top talent. Designing a space that supports employee well-being, promotes collaboration, and facilitates productivity ensures your team remains engaged and committed to your business's success. A well-designed workspace can also contribute to higher levels of job satisfaction, reducing staff turnover and fostering a strong company culture.

Investing in your property also signals to your employees that you're dedicated to their long-term growth and development. By providing a stable and supportive work environment, you demonstrate your commitment to their career advancement, leading to increased loyalty and a stronger team.

Your local business should also be perceived as a long-term part of the community. When you invest in owning your commercial space, you're demonstrating to your customers that you're dedicated to their needs and the local community's well-being. This commitment can lead to increased trust, goodwill, and a positive reputation that ultimately results in more business opportunities and growth.

Moving Forward: Tax Benefits and Beyond

To summarize, owning your commercial space offers you the freedom and autonomy to make decisions that best serve your business without the constraints of dealing with a landlord. This control allows you to navigate the challenges of running a successful enterprise with confidence, knowing that your property's future is in your hands.

By eliminating the uncertainties and restrictions associated with leasing, you can focus your energy and resources on growing your business, building lasting relationships with your customers and employees, and creating a stable foundation for continued success.

As we move into the next chapter, we'll delve into the substantial tax benefits that come with owning and how you can leverage these advantages to keep more of your hard-earned money. By understanding the financial incentives associated with property ownership, you can make informed decisions that maximize your business's potential and secure a prosperous future for you and your employees.

Chapter 6

Outfoxing the Taxman: Wise Moves & Wins

"In this world, nothing can be said to be certain, except death and taxes."

- Benjamin Franklin.

As a successful business owner, you've likely experienced the bittersweet reality of increased profits leading to a more significant tax burden. While it's only fair to pay your share of taxes, it's essential to ensure that your hard-earned money isn't unnecessarily slipping through your fingers.

The truth is, the more successful you become, the more the tax man wants a piece of your pie. It may feel like you're being penalized for your accomplishments, and that's a tough pill to swallow. After all, you've taken significant risks, invested countless hours, and created job opportunities for many people to build your business.

It's easy to fall into the trap of feeling powerless against the tax system.

You may even question whether your success is worth the increased tax burden. But the reality is that taxes are a part of life, and the key is to understand and navigate the system in your favor. The wealthy and successful have long employed various strategies to minimize their taxes legally, and there's no reason you shouldn't do the same.

This chapter will explore these strategies and show you that there's no need to let the tax man be your number one enemy. You have the power to take control of your financial destiny and ensure that you're not paying more than necessary.

We'll delve into the world of depreciation, a powerful tool for reducing your taxable income when owning commercial property. Also, we'll discuss ways to leverage your equity without incurring immediate tax consequences, helping you build wealth for your family and future generations.

By understanding and implementing these strategies, you can minimize your tax burden, keep more of your hard-earned money, and continue to grow your business without fear of being penalized for your success. As you embark on this journey, remember that the goal isn't to evade taxes, but rather to ensure that you're not paying more than you have to. With the right knowledge and guidance, you can level the playing field and navigate the tax system with confidence.

Two Businesses, One Goal: Creative and Legal Tax Reduction Strategies

Owning the building where your business operates presents a unique opportunity to effectively manage two businesses: your primary business and the real estate that it lives in. This dual-business structure offers creative and legal ways to reduce your taxable income, allowing you to retain more of your hard-earned money.

One strategy is to set up a separate legal entity for the real estate, such as a limited liability company (LLC) or a corporation[4]. This entity can be the landlord to your primary business, which leases the space for its operations. By structuring it this way, you can allocate expenses and income between the two businesses to maximize tax benefits.

For example, you can charge your primary business a fair market rent, which will be an expense for your primary business and income for your real estate business. This allows you to offset expenses in your real estate business against the rental income, potentially reducing your overall taxable income.

---

[4] Do not construe this as direct legal or tax advice. Every situation is different. Please consult licensed legal and tax professionals for specific advice and counsel.

Let's explore an example to better understand this strategy. Suppose you own a roofing company, we'll call it "Roofing Today". You've recently purchased a building to house your operations. You decide to set up an LLC for the building itself, which we'll call "535 Main Street", and it will lease the space to your roofing business. Roofing Today will pay rent to 535 Main Street, LLC at a fair market rate. This rent payment is a tax-deductible expense for your roofing business, effectively reducing its taxable income. At the same time, the rental income received by your real estate holding company, 535 Main Street LLC, would be considered income for that entity. The good news is you can reduce 535 Main Street's taxable income by various expenses that it incurs on its own, such as mortgage interest, property taxes, insurance, and maintenance costs.

By strategically managing income and expenses between your two businesses, you can minimize your overall tax burden.

This dual-business strategy not only provides tax benefits but also helps protect your assets by separating the liabilities of your primary business and the real estate. In the event of a lawsuit or financial difficulties, having separate legal entities can limit the exposure of one business to the liabilities of the other.

Depreciation: A Powerful Tool for Reducing Taxable Income

Depreciation is a tax deduction that allows property owners to recover the costs associated with acquiring and improving their commercial real estate. By understanding and leveraging depreciation, you can significantly reduce your taxable income, enabling you to retain more of your profits for reinvestment or personal use.

Depreciation is based on the idea that an asset, such as a commercial property, loses value over time due to wear and tear, aging, and other factors. The Internal Revenue Service (IRS) allows property owners to deduct a portion of the property's cost each year over a predetermined period, known as the property's "useful life." For commercial buildings, the IRS typically assigns a useful life of 39 years under the Modified Accelerated Cost Recovery System (Publication 946)[5], during which you can claim annual depreciation deductions.

To maximize the benefits of depreciation, it's essential to understand the different types of depreciation available for commercial properties. The two main types are straight-line depreciation and cost segregation.

---

[5] United States, Internal Revenue Service. *How To Depreciate Property*. Publication 946, 2022. https://www.irs.gov/publications/p946

1. **Straight-line depreciation:** This is the most common method of calculating depreciation for commercial properties. With this method, you simply divide the building's cost (minus the land value) by its useful life (39 years for commercial properties). You can then deduct this annual amount from your taxable income each year over the property's useful life.

2. **Cost segregation:** This advanced depreciation strategy[6] involves identifying and separating the various components of your property into different asset classes with shorter useful lives. By doing so, you can accelerate depreciation deductions, resulting in significant tax savings in the early years of property ownership. Cost segregation requires a specialized study conducted by a qualified professional, but the potential tax savings can be well worth the investment.

Let's consider a simple example to illustrate the power of depreciation. Imagine you've purchased a commercial building for $1.25 million, and the value of the land is $250,000. Using straight-line depreciation, you can

---

[6] United States, Internal Revenue Service. *Cost Segregation Audit Technique Guide.* 2022

deduct $25,641 ($1,000,000 / 39 years) from your taxable income each year. If you're in the 35% tax bracket, this annual depreciation deduction translates to tax savings of approximately $8,974 per year.

Now, let's say you decide to invest in a cost segregation study and find that 20% of the building's value can be allocated to assets with a shorter useful life of 15 years. In this case, you can accelerate the depreciation deductions for this portion of the building's value, resulting in even greater tax savings during the first 15 years of ownership.

Depreciation is a powerful tool that allows commercial property owners to reduce their taxable income and keep more of their profits. By understanding and strategically leveraging depreciation, you can maximize your tax savings, invest in your business's growth, and create a brighter financial future.

Harness the Power of Equity to Fuel Growth and Wealth without Immediate Tax Consequences

Equity, the difference between the market value of your commercial property and the outstanding mortgage balance, is a valuable asset that can be strategically utilized to fuel the growth and wealth of your business without incurring immediate tax consequences. By tapping into this powerful financial resource, you can unlock a world of possibilities for expansion, investment, and securing the financial future of your family and future generations.

There are several ways to leverage the equity in your commercial property without triggering a taxable event:

1. **You can cash-out refinance:** A cash-out refinance involves replacing your existing mortgage with a new, larger loan, allowing you to access the difference in cash. This cash can be used for various purposes, such as reinvesting in your business, purchasing additional properties, or funding other investments. The interest on the new loan may be tax-deductible, and the cash you receive from the refinance is generally not considered taxable income.

2. **You can secure a commercial line of credit:** A commercial line of credit is a flexible financing option that provides access to funds based on the equity in your commercial property. You can use this credit for working capital, inventory acquisition, or other business-related expenses. Interest on the borrowed funds may be tax-deductible, and the funds you access through the commercial line of credit are not considered taxable income.

3. **You can execute a 1031 exchange:** A 1031 exchange, also known as a like-kind exchange, allows you to defer taxes on the sale of your commercial property by reinvesting the proceeds into a similar, or more expensive, qualifying property[7]. By doing this, you can grow your real estate portfolio and defer the capital gains taxes associated with the sale, allowing you to leverage your equity to expand your wealth without incurring an immediate tax liability.

4. **You can enhance your estate planning and generational wealth transfer:** By owning commercial property, you can pass on a valuable asset to future generations, potentially avoiding or minimizing estate taxes through proper planning. This can ensure that your family continues to benefit from your success and hard work, even after you're gone.

Leveraging the equity in your commercial property without incurring immediate tax consequences is an essential aspect of building wealth and creating long-term

---

[7] Hahn, Amanda, and Matthew Macfarland. *The Book on Tax Strategies for the Savvy Real Estate Investor: Powerful techniques anyone can use to deduct more, invest smarter, and pay far less to the IRS!* BiggerPockets; First Edition. 2016

financial stability. By understanding the various strategies available to you and working with trusted legal, financial and tax professionals, you can harness the power of equity to fuel your business's growth, invest in new opportunities, and secure a prosperous future for you and your family.

As we transition to the next chapter, we will tackle the critical question of how to identify the ideal space for your business. We'll discuss how to evaluate your present and future needs, ensuring that your commercial property serves as a solid foundation for your ongoing success.

Chapter 7

Spot Check: Location as Your Ace Card

"The three most important things in property: Location, location, location."
- Lord Harold Samuel

As a successful business owner, one of the critical decisions you'll need to make is choosing the right property for your operations. Your business's location and space can significantly impact its growth and overall success. This chapter will explore the essential factors to consider when searching for the ideal property to accommodate your present and future needs. We'll also discuss how to approach potential compromises, work with a commercial real estate agent, and set the stage for financing your dream property.

But first, let's consider the story of Robbie and Mark, two ambitious college friends and aspiring entrepreneurs who were determined to build a successful business. Their inspiration stemmed from one of the world's most iconic companies, McDonald's, which was widely known for creating the fast-food revolution. Those with insider knowledge, however, recognized that McDonald's real success lay in its strategic acquisition of prime real estate, not in food service..

Intrigued by this business model, Robbie and Mark decided to follow a similar strategy but with a twist. They chose to pursue the car wash industry instead, believing it to be a lucrative venture due to its evergreen demand, low labor requirements, and the ability to establish locations in high-traffic areas.

Their master plan was to create a chain of car washes with the primary focus on owning the real estate on which the businesses operated. The car washes would generate the income necessary to pay for the properties, which would appreciate over time, thereby increasing the overall value of their enterprise.

The pair understood that location would be king and their success hinged on choosing carefully selected sites that matched a predefined set of key attributes and qualities. They foresaw that it wasn't just about operating a chain of car washes, but also owning the underlying real estate.

With this master plan, their vision extended beyond the immediate cash flow from the car washes. Each location was chosen meticulously, ensuring it had the potential for high customer traffic and strong future appreciation. The car washes served a dual-purpose strategy: generating the income to cover the property costs while simultaneously building wealth as the property values rose.

A decade plus later, Robbie and Mark's vision had materialized. They successfully built and managed a series of car washes, each strategically located on valuable real estate. Their decision to own the land beneath their businesses proved to be a game-changer, as it significantly contributed to their financial success. And as their enterprise grew, they expanded their vision to realize how profitable the actual operating companies could become - which to them was an eye-opening serendipity.

When they eventually decided to sell the bulk of their enterprise, the value of the real estate played a pivotal role in securing a substantial sum.

Robbie and Mark's story is a testament to the power of envisioning and executing a well-thought-out plan and being strategic about location. By recognizing the immense potential in merging a profitable business with valuable real estate investments, they created a winning formula that continues to inspire entrepreneurs worldwide.

Start With A Vision Of Your Ideal Property

Taking the time to thoroughly analyze your present and future needs is critical when searching for the perfect property for your business. This process involves considering various factors such as location, size, layout, and potential for growth. Each aspect plays a significant role in shaping your business operations, employee satisfaction, and customer experience.

Location is a crucial factor, as it can determine your business's visibility, accessibility, and potential customer base. Consider whether you need a location in a high-traffic area, or whether you require easy access to public transportation and parking for your employees and customers. Investigate the surrounding area for competitors, potential partners, and other relevant businesses that may impact your company's success. Additionally, look at the local demographics to ensure that your target market is well-represented in the vicinity.

You need to also understand the local zoning regulations when you're trying to pick the perfect spot for your business. Zoning laws decide how you can use a piece of land, and they can vary widely from one town to the next. By getting the lowdown on these rules, you'll make sure your business fits right in, avoiding any legal headaches or expensive fines later on. Plus, knowing the ins and outs of zoning can help you spot opportunities for growing your business, since it tells you what types of businesses are allowed in certain areas.

Size is another essential aspect to consider. Your property should have sufficient space to accommodate your current operations, employees, and equipment. However, it's also vital to think about potential growth and expansion. Assess whether the property can support future increases in staff, additional equipment, or changes in your business model. This forward-thinking approach will help ensure that your property remains suitable for your business as it evolves.

The layout of your property can have a substantial impact on your business's overall functionality and efficiency. Consider whether you need an open-plan space, individual offices, or a combination of both. Think about storage needs, meeting areas, and any specialized rooms or facilities your business might require. If your company relies on specific machinery or equipment, ensure that the property can accommodate these items and their necessary infrastructure.

Deciding between building new or renovating an existing property is another critical consideration. If you choose to build new, you'll have greater control over the design and layout to suit your business's unique needs. However, this option typically involves a more significant investment of time and money. On the other hand, renovating an existing property can be more cost-effective and time-efficient, but may require compromises in terms of design and functionality.

Involving key stakeholders in the decision-making process can help ensure a well-rounded perspective on your business's needs. Consult with managers, employees, and even customers to gather insights and identify any specific requirements that should be addressed.

It is also essential to establish a clear budget before starting your search. Having a predefined budget will help narrow down your options and prevent financial strain on your business.

In summary, thoroughly understanding your business's present and future needs is crucial to identifying the ideal property. Consider the importance of location, size, layout, and the potential for growth or renovation. Engage with stakeholders, and establish a clear budget to ensure that your search for the perfect property is efficient, focused, and ultimately successful.

You Must Accept That the "Perfect" Location Might Not Exist

When searching for the ideal commercial property, it's essential to acknowledge that finding the "perfect" location is likely an unrealistic expectation. Accepting this fact early in the process will help prevent frustration and enable you to focus on what truly matters; securing a property that effectively meets your business's needs and priorities. By embracing compromises and being open to various options, you can better navigate the process and find a suitable location that aligns with your objectives.

One key aspect to consider is your timeline. The process of finding, purchasing, and preparing a commercial property for your business can be lengthy, and you may encounter unexpected challenges along the way. Accepting that the perfect location might not be immediately available can help you remain patient and focused during this process. Be prepared to adapt your timeline as needed, and remember that flexibility can be crucial in securing a suitable property.

Budget is another area where you may need to compromise. While it's crucial to establish a budget early in the process, you may find that the properties meeting all your criteria are outside of your price range. In these situations, it's essential to prioritize your business's needs and determine which aspects are most critical. By focusing on the most important factors and being open to compromise on others, you can find a property that aligns with your business's priorities and financial constraints.

Embracing the inevitability of compromise is an essential aspect of the commercial property search process. By acknowledging that the perfect location might not exist, you can focus on the properties that align with your business's priorities, even if they require some adjustments. Being open to different options, understanding zoning implications, and adapting your timeline and budget as needed will ultimately help you find a suitable property that supports your business's growth and success.

You Can Simplify the Process

The process of finding the right commercial property for your business can seem daunting, but it doesn't have to be difficult. By partnering with a knowledgeable commercial real estate agent, you can significantly simplify the process and increase your chances of finding the ideal property. Additionally, our company has developed an extensive network of professional and successful commercial realtors, and we're more than happy to recommend one that will suit your needs and preferences.

Commercial real estate agents are experts in their field, and they possess valuable insights and experience that can help you navigate the complexities of the commercial property market. They can assist in identifying suitable properties, conducting market research, and negotiating favorable terms. By working with a professional, you can save time, avoid potential pitfalls, and ensure that you secure a property that aligns with your business's needs and priorities.

One critical advantage of partnering with a commercial agent is their deep understanding of the local market. Agents generally have substantial knowledge of the area in which they operate, including zoning regulations, property values, and market trends. This information can be invaluable in guiding your search and helping you make informed decisions.

Furthermore, a commercial real estate agent can help you assess and prioritize your property needs. They can assist in determining the size, location, and features that are most important for your business's success. By working with an expert, you can ensure that you focus on the most critical aspects and avoid getting sidetracked by less significant details.

One of the most important benefits of working with a commercial agent is the negotiation skills and the unemotional engagement they bring when it's time to present an offer on a property. They can help you secure favorable terms on your purchase, potentially saving you thousands of dollars in the long run. By having a professional advocate for your interests, you can ensure that you're getting the best possible deal.

Deciding when to engage an agent depends on your specific needs and circumstances. However, it's generally a good idea to involve one early in the process. This will allow them to help you with every stage of the property search, from identifying potential properties to closing the deal. Additionally, in most cases, the agent is paid directly by the seller, not you, so there's no reason to not engage with the best.

In conclusion, working with a commercial real estate agent can greatly simplify the process of finding the right commercial property for your business. They bring valuable expertise and local market knowledge to the table, helping you navigate the complexities of the market, prioritize your needs, and secure favorable terms.

As a company, we're proud of the extensive network of professional and successful commercial realtors we've built, and we're confident that we can recommend an agent that will help you find the perfect property for your business.

As we move on to the next chapter, we'll explore the financial considerations and options for acquiring a commercial property, which might be the most crucial aspect of the process.

Our company has developed a proven, time-tested process that will help you secure the *right* financing for your acquisition, rather than just *any* financing. With countless options available, navigating the commercial property financing landscape can be complex and confusing. But rest assured, with our expert guidance, you'll have the support and direction you need to make the best decisions for your business and your future. So, let's dive into the world of financing and discover the path to success in acquiring the perfect commercial space for your business.

Chapter 8

Funding Your Fortress: The Financial Labyrinth

"Give me six hours to chop down a tree and I will spend the first four sharpening the ax." - Abraham Lincoln

Picture this: you've finally found the perfect commercial property to house your growing business. It's everything you've been searching for, and now it's time to make it yours. But there's one critical step that stands between you and your dream space – securing the right financing. This is where the rubber meets the road, and where many business owners stumble.

Why? Because navigating the complex world of commercial lending can feel like traversing a minefield. Missteps here could result in the loss of your dream property. The road to securing financing is littered with potential pitfalls, but with the right knowledge and guidance, you can avoid these traps and emerge victorious. In this chapter,

First, we'll explore the overall financing process – why it's essential to understand the ins and outs, what's involved, and how to navigate this complex landscape. This knowledge will empower you to approach the process with confidence and a clear understanding of what's required to secure the funds you need.

Next, we'll delve into the vast chasm between commercial and residential lending. These two worlds may seem similar on the surface, but they're as different as night and day. I'll explain what sets commercial lending apart and why it's crucial to understand these distinctions as you search for the perfect financing solution.

Finally, we'll discuss the importance of getting your financial house in order. Your financials are the foundation upon which your commercial lending success is built, and without a solid foundation, your dreams could come crashing down. I'll reveal how to get your financials borrower-ready and ensure you're prepared to face even the most discerning underwriter or loan committee.

With the right tools, knowledge, and guidance, you'll be well on your way to securing the funds you need to make your dream commercial space a reality.

Start With The High Level View

Imagine standing at the base of a towering mountain, staring up at the peak that seems impossibly far away. The climb may appear daunting, even insurmountable, but with the right map, gear, and guidance, you can conquer that summit and claim your rightful place at the top. The same principle applies to the process of securing financing for your commercial property – with the right knowledge, preparation, and guidance, you can overcome any obstacle and achieve your goal.

But why is understanding the financing process so crucial to your success? The answer is simple: knowledge is power. When you comprehend the intricacies of the commercial lending landscape, you can approach it with confidence, armed with the information you need to negotiate favorable terms and secure the funds necessary to acquire your ideal commercial space. So, what does this process entail, and who's involved?

First, it's essential to recognize that the commercial lending process is a complex, multifaceted endeavor, often involving multiple parties, including lenders, brokers, appraisers, attorneys, and more. Each player has a role to play, and understanding how these pieces fit together is key to navigating the process with ease.

Next, it's crucial to know when to begin this journey. Waiting until you've found the perfect property is a recipe for disaster – by the time you've secured financing, that ideal space may have slipped through your fingers. Instead, start the process early, researching lenders, gathering documentation, and laying the groundwork for a successful financing experience.

Where do you begin this monumental undertaking? Start by building a solid foundation of knowledge, familiarizing yourself with the various lending options available to you, and understanding the unique requirements and considerations of each. This knowledge will enable you to identify the best financing solution for your specific needs, and position you as an informed, savvy borrower in the eyes of potential lenders.

The journey to securing financing for your property may seem long and arduous, but with the right understanding of the process, you can navigate the twists and turns with confidence and grace. Let's continue our ascent, armed with the knowledge and determination to conquer the financing mountain and claim our prize at the summit.

Understand How Commercial Lending Is Much Different Than Residential Lending

If you've ever purchased a home, you have experienced first hand the residential side of real estate lending. Most people get a 15 or 30 year fixed-rate loan, and essentially the only variables that matter are your interest rate, down payment required and loan fees. Occasionally people choose something a bit more out of the mainstream, like an adjustable rate, but that is generally pretty rare and only makes sense in limited situations.

Yes, residential underwriters take a deep dive look at your ability to repay and your personal credit, but that's about as far as it goes. Residential lending is highly regulated and standardized by the "agencies" - Fannie Mae and Freddie Mac - which are quasi-government organizations that to a large extent make the rules that everyone follows. So the loan "terms" that you find from one lender or broker to another will be very close in most situations.

But what makes commercial lending so different from residential lending, and why is it vital to grasp these distinctions? The stakes are higher, the rules are more complex, and the players are much more specialized. Unlike residential lending, which is primarily focused on the borrower's personal creditworthiness, commercial lending takes a more comprehensive approach, considering additional factors such as the property type, its potential cash flow, location, and even the industry in which your business operates.

In addition to considering many more factors in the approval process, each lender will often make unique requirements in order to fund your loan. For instance, many banks will require you to move a substantial amount of your bank deposits to their institution as a condition to fund your loan. They may require you to sign onerous "covenants", which can dictate conditions you must agree to follow even after your loan funds. One example would be requiring you to submit your business financials yearly after loan approval to insure that your business is still healthy. Some loans will require full personal guarantees, while others may not. Interest rates are generally not fixed for the entire loan term like residential loans are, although some can be.

As a savvy entrepreneur , it's essential to recognize these distinctions and adapt your strategy accordingly. By understanding the unique challenges and considerations of commercial lending, you can position yourself as an informed, strategic borrower, capable of securing the best possible financing terms for your property.

So, where do you find the right financing for your needs? It's crucial to cast a wide net, exploring a diverse array of lending options – from traditional banks and credit unions to alternative lenders, such as private equity firms and hard money lenders. Each option has its own set of advantages and disadvantages, and understanding these nuances is key to determining the best fit for your unique circumstances. In addition, many of the best sources will not be located in your backyard.

However, you don't have to go it alone. Enlisting the help of seasoned professionals, such as a competent commercial mortgage broker, can give you the edge you need to navigate the complex world of commercial lending successfully. These experts have the knowledge, experience, and connections necessary to guide you through the process, ensuring that you secure the best possible financing for your acquisition.

In the game of commercial lending, understanding the rules is essential to achieving victory. By unraveling the mysteries of this complex world, you can position yourself as a shrewd, strategic player, armed with the knowledge and insight necessary to secure the financing you need to make your dream commercial property a reality. Are you ready to take your seat at the table and play to win?

The Power of Preparation: Unlocking Your Financial Potential and Seizing Success

Having your financial records in order is critical, and it can make or break your success. Your records serve as a roadmap to your business's financial history and current health, guiding lenders as they evaluate your eligibility for financing. A well-organized, comprehensive set of financials demonstrates your competence, responsibility, and commitment to success – all qualities that lenders seek in a borrower.

So how can you ensure that your business financials are borrower-ready? Begin by gathering key documents, such as your current year-to-date profit and loss statement and balance sheet, and tax returns (both business and personal) for the past three years. Review these records for accuracy and consistency, addressing any discrepancies or red flags. Consider working with a trusted financial advisor or CPA to help you analyze them and identify areas for improvement.

One critical aspect of financial preparation is understanding the concept of "global cashflow". By assessing your global cashflow, lenders can determine your ability to manage the added financial responsibilities that come with owning commercial property. This comprehensive measure of your financial health takes into account not only your business's income and expenses but also your personal finances.

Know that the global cashflow consideration process considers all of your income sources. If you have a 20% or more ownership interest in any business outside of your primary enterprise, you will also need to provide financials on that business. Lenders are smart and know that one business may affect another.

One of the key documents in this process that you may not be familiar with is the Personal Financial Statement

(PFS). All commercial lending sources will require this. It is essentially a document that summarizes your personal financial health - your income, expenses, assets and debts. Think of it as your *personal* "profit and loss" statement and "balance sheet" wrapped into one document.

Many people make the mistake of being casual about or inflating numbers on these documents, and it creates problems for them later in the loan process. You'll want to be straightforward, honest and accurate as lenders consider this document to be a reflection of your character. I've seen more than one deal get derailed late in the game because the business owner *forgot* to add some property or liability that they had, or overinflated their net worth.

Know that accuracy is important as the lender will use data from your PFS in the approval process. For instance, they are going to look closely at your cash and cash equivalents to evaluate what kind of capacity you have for your down payment on the loan. And what kind of reserves you'll have remaining after your loan closes as a "safety-net" to cover the unexpected.

Determining affordability is another essential piece of the puzzle, both from your perspective and that of the lender. This involves assessing your current and projected income, evaluating your global debt service coverage ratio, and considering factors such as interest rates and loan terms. By understanding your financial capacity, you can make informed decisions about the size and scope of the commercial property you can realistically afford.

In the quest for commercial property ownership, the power of preparation cannot be underestimated. By getting your financial documents in order and understanding the intricacies of global cashflow and affordability, you can unlock the vault of opportunity, seizing the rewards that await you on the other side.

In the next chapter, we'll delve deeper into the crucial elements that shape your financial options, unearthing the secrets to success that only the most savvy entrepreneurs know. We will explore the Big Three legs of the lending stool: credit, collateral, and cashflow. These three powerful forces hold the key to unlocking the best financing opportunities for your commercial property.

Chapter 9

Decoding Dollars: Navigate Lending Like a Pro

"The beginning of wisdom is the definition of terms." - Socrates

The power to unlock a world of new opportunities is within your grasp, but only if you can master the essential components of the lending game. The secret to this success lies in understanding the three critical pillars of lending: **credit**, **collateral**, and **cashflow**. These pillars, when harnessed effectively, can catapult your commercial property investment journey into the realm of extraordinary success.

In this chapter, we will unravel the mysteries behind these three pillars and reveal how you can use them to your advantage, opening the door to more favorable loan terms, lower interest rates, and a stronger financial foundation. We'll explore the types and importance of your credit history, the undeniable value of collateral, and the lifeblood of your business that is cashflow – all of which are vital components in securing the best possible financing options for your investment.

Credit: How Your Financial Character Holds the Key to Boundless Opportunities

Imagine the financial world as a stage, with you as the protagonist. In this grand performance, your credit score plays the role of your reputation – the way you are perceived by the audience of potential lenders, partners, and investors. But what exactly is credit, and how does it relate to your character?

Credit, at its core, is a reflection of your financial persona. It is a measure of your trustworthiness and responsibility when it comes to handling money, both personally and professionally. In the eyes of the financial world, your credit score acts as a beacon that signals your credibility and creditworthiness.

There are two primary types of credit scores: personal and business. While your personal credit score represents your individual financial history, your business credit score pertains to the creditworthiness of your company. Both scores are crucial, as they can impact your ability to secure loans and favorable financing terms for your commercial property investments.

Why is good credit so paramount? By maintaining a strong credit score, you send a clear message to the financial world that you are a reliable and trustworthy borrower. This, in turn, can unlock a treasure trove of opportunities, such as competitive loan terms and lower interest rates, which can significantly boost your investment journey.

Conversely, bad credit can be a costly burden that hampers your financial progress. A poor credit score can limit your access to financing options, result in higher interest rates, and hinder your ability to secure the funds necessary for your property endeavors. In essence, bad credit can be an Achilles' heel that threatens to undermine your financial aspirations.

Realize too that with the explosion of the internet and social media, lenders are now seriously reviewing and considering what your customers and others are saying about you. *Noone wants to lend money to a company that treats its customers poorly[8].*

Every business has bad reviews from time to time, but a history of unhappy and unresolved customer issues does not bode favorably for you in most lender's eyes. Work to earn the best reviews, and try to use every customer complaint as an opportunity to resolve and turn them into an advocate.

---

[8] This can be a real, tangible drag on a company's ability to secure credit.

Know that having good credit and character are essential components of your financial success. The good news is that your credit score is not set in stone. By adopting smart financial habits and nurturing both your personal and business credit scores, you can gradually elevate your financial standing and unlock a world of opportunities that were once out of reach.

Collateral: Harnessing the Potential of Your Assets for Favorable Loan Terms

What exactly is collateral, and why is it so vital to your financial journey? Collateral is a tangible asset that you pledge to a lender as a form of security for a loan. In the event that you default on the loan, the lender has the right to seize the collateral to recoup their losses. By offering collateral, you are providing the lender with a safety net, which can significantly improve your chances of securing favorable loan terms and interest rates.

From a lender's perspective, not all assets are created equally. Typically, lenders are looking for assets that are easily valued and can be readily liquidated in case of loan default. Examples of collateral that are often accepted by lenders include real estate, vehicles, and equipment. On the other hand, assets such as artwork, collectibles, or speculative investments will not be considered acceptable by most lenders due to their volatile or subjective nature.

The power of collateral lies in its ability to create a win-win scenario for both you and the lender. By offering a valuable asset as security, you demonstrate your commitment to repaying the loan and instill confidence in the lender's decision to finance your property investment. This, in turn, can lead to more favorable loan terms, lower interest rates, and access to larger loan amounts – all of which can significantly impact your financial success. Think about it this way. Would you loan your own money to someone who had no downside risk in a venture if it went sideways? Wouldn't you want a way to recapture your money?

The good news here is that the piece of commercial real estate you acquire will be the primary source of collateral for the lender, but they will also want you to have some of your own skin in the game. This generally starts with your down payment, or equity injection, and the larger that percentage is, the more comfortable typical lenders will be with your deal. In some cases, though, you can mitigate a larger down payment with other sources of collateral.

It's necessary to approach collateral with a strategic mindset. You will want to carefully evaluate the assets you plan to use as collateral, considering their value, liquidity, and the potential risks involved. By doing so, you can make informed decisions that will maximize the benefits of collateral while minimizing any potential pitfalls.

Cashflow: The Lifeblood of Your Financial Empire and How Lenders View It

Imagine a mighty river, its waters flowing ceaselessly, nurturing the lands and sustaining life in its path. In the world of commercial property investing, cashflow is that river – the lifeblood of your financial empire, coursing through its veins, powering its growth, and breathing life into your dreams of wealth and prosperity.

But what is cashflow, and why is it so vital to your financial journey? It refers to the net amount of money moving in and out of your business or personal finances. It's the fuel that powers your financial engine, allowing you to seize opportunities, invest in growth, and navigate the tumultuous waters of the market with confidence and agility.

From a lender's perspective, there are two types of cashflow: business and global. Business cashflow refers to the money generated by your primary business operations. In contrast, global cashflow encompasses all of your income sources, including rental income, investments, and other financial assets. Lenders often evaluate both types of cashflow to determine your ability to repay a loan and assess the overall health of your financial domain.

Lenders will be focused on evaluating your business's debt service coverage ratio (DSCR) to determine if you will have the operating margin necessary to successfully manage the new building debt over the long run. This is simply the idea of dividing your net operating income by your minimum debt service obligations. They typically want to see a ratio of 1.25, which means your net income is 125% greater than your debt service payments. There are variations to this number, but it is a good general minimum guideline for financial health.

Mastering the art of cashflow management and optimization is essential for your financial success. Here are some strategies to improve your cashflow and strengthen your financial foundation:

1. **Optimize your expenses:** Keep a close eye on your expenses and identify areas where you can cut costs without sacrificing the quality of your products or services. By reducing unnecessary expenses, you can boost your cashflow and direct those funds toward growth initiatives.

2. **Increase your revenue streams:** Diversify your income sources to create a more resilient cashflow. This might involve expanding your product or service offerings, tapping into new markets, or investing in complementary businesses. Or, consider raising your prices.

Most small businesses cannot compete with Amazon and the biggies on being the lowest price, but too many try.

3. **Manage your debt strategically:** While debt can be a useful tool for growth and expansion, it can also weigh heavily on your cashflow if not managed effectively. Develop a plan to pay down or refinance high-interest debt as quickly as possible, and carefully consider the terms and conditions of any new debt you take on.

By optimizing and increasing your cashflow you can unlock the full potential of your financial empire, fueling its growth, and propelling it toward unprecedented success. Many entrepreneurs get nervous or insecure when thinking about the financial numbers of their business and prefer to bury their heads in the sand, but you should embrace the power of knowing the truth. Your cashflow tells a story about your business, and can give you valuable insights to leverage effective changes bringing you ever closer to the realm of wealth and prosperity that you so richly deserve.

As we transition to the next chapter, we'll delve deeper into the pros and cons of specific financing options and how the three legs of the lending stool can impact those choices. You'll be better equipped to make strategic decisions that will ensure your financial progress continues to advance forward in an ever-evolving market.

Chapter 10

Loan Wisdom:
Know to Grow Your Wealth

"Risk comes from not knowing what you're doing." – Warren Buffett

Let me tell you about my buddy, Nathan. He's a real go-getter, running his own small trucking company for the past six years. His setup is pretty slick. He's got a fleet of five trucks and operators, all strategically located right by the seaport. Their bread and butter? Moving cargo from those massive ships that dock in and out of the port to local staging areas or warehouses. Sometimes they deliver the cargo locally, and sometimes they just set it up for the long haul truckers to take it the rest of the way.

After a few years, Nathan realized he was letting a ton of profit slip right through his fingers. His customers were forking out big bucks for storing their goods while they were waiting to be transported or moved further down the line. And this cash was just whizzing straight through Nathan's hands. He thought, "Hang on a minute, I can capture all of this!" He saw a golden opportunity to expand his business.

So he found a warehouse located about 20 minutes from his main company headquarters, but still conveniently located by the port. Now, instead of watching all that revenue zoom off to a third-party, he could bring it home, significantly boosting his bottom line. Pretty clever, right? What a win for Nathan!

But then he hit a roadblock. He walked into his trusted local bank, the one he'd been banking with for years. But instead of helping him capture this golden opportunity, they gave him just one option to consider. To make things worse, they demanded a hefty downpayment. Sure, Nathan had the cash, but he didn't want to drain all of his working capital reserves. He needed to keep the engine of his business running smoothly and liked the idea of keeping some reserve cash for a rainy day. It was a real head-scratcher, and not the kind of help he was expecting from his long-time bank.

Embarking on the journey of buying an owner-occupied commercial space is a thrilling endeavor, but it's essential to remember that there's more to it than merely finding the perfect property. An essential part of your success lies in securing the right financial solution to make your dream happen. We will now explore the world of financing options, how the market can change, and the importance of making an informed decision.

The Myriad of Loan Options — A Deeper Dive

Understanding the vast array of loan options available to you is central to making an informed decision. Here are some of the most common loan types and their unique features.

1. **SBA 7A Loans:** These loans, backed by the Small Business Administration (SBA)[9], offer attractive terms and interest rates for small business owners. SBA 7A loans can be used for various purposes, including purchasing or refinancing owner-occupied commercial real estate. They typically come with longer repayment terms and lower down payment requirements, making them an excellent choice for businesses looking to minimize upfront costs.

2. **SBA 504 Loans:** Like the 7A loans, SBA 504 loans are designed to support small businesses. However, 504 loans specifically target commercial real estate purchases and major

---

[9] U.S. Small Business Administration. "SOP 10 7: Standard Operating Procedure for Small Business Loans." August 1, 2023. U.S. Small Business Administration, https://www.sba.gov/document/sop-50-10-lender-development-company-loan-programs

equipment acquisitions. They provide long-term, fixed-rate financing with lower down payment requirements. SBA 504 loans are a solid option for businesses looking to invest in their commercial property without breaking the bank. Prepayment penalties on 504 loans are generally higher and run longer than on 7A loans.

*A quick note on SBA loans: All SBA lenders are **not** created equally. By definition, all federally chartered banks can write an SBA-guaranteed loan, but most are simply not good at it. Most banks only fund a small number of these types of loans each year - not enough to be effective at it as the process can be complex. In addition, most banks are not classified as "preferred" SBA PLP lenders, which means after the bank approves your loan, they have to send it to the SBA for some governmental bureaucrat to review and re-underwrite. This can make the process about as fast as a turtle. A PLP lender, on the other hand, has full underwriting and funding authority granted by the Small Business Administration. These lenders specialize in SBA funding and can make the final approval decision without the need for feedback or delays from the SBA at all. This makes the process much more consistent, efficient and fast.*

3. **Conventional Bank Loans:** These loans are provided by traditional banks and are not backed by the SBA. Conventional loans may come with more stringent qualification requirements and shorter repayment terms, but they can offer competitive interest rates for well-qualified borrowers. With a strong financial track record and a solid business plan, conventional bank loans can be a viable financing option.

4. **No-Doc Loans:** No-doc (or no documentation) loans are designed for borrowers who may not have the traditional documentation required for other loan types. These loans often come with higher interest rates and may require larger down payments, but they can be an attractive option for borrowers with strong credit and substantial assets who want to bypass the standard documentation process.

5. **Lite-Doc Loans:** Similar to no-doc loans, lite-doc loans require less documentation than traditional loans. Borrowers with strong credit and assets may qualify for lite-doc loans, which typically come with slightly lower interest rates than no-doc loans. This loan type can be an appealing option for those looking for a more streamlined lending process.

By exploring the various loan types available and understanding their unique features, you can better assess which financing solution is best suited for your business's needs. Th e right choice will depend on factors such as your "Big Three" (credit, collateral and cashflow), business plan, and financial standing. By carefully considering these factors and weighing the pros and cons of each loan type, you'll be better equipped to make an informed decision and set your business on the path to success.

Back to the story of my friend Nathan. He discovered the difficult lesson that many entrepreneurs and business owners learn, and in many cases sadly when it's too late. The simple lesson is this: the *bank is not your friend.*

Yes, they spend millions of dollars promoting the idea that they are "business friendly" and that their entire reason for existence is to help small businesses succeed. But that's just a masquerade. Let me tell you who their **real** customers are:

1. The bank regulators
2. Their board of directors
3. Their shareholders

Not you. You are a necessary inconvenience, and a way, when it works for them, to increase their profits with as little risk as possible. And the larger the bank, the worse they generally are for you as a small business owner.

Not only will they offer you limited options that fit into their portfolio appetite of the day, but they will also want your business banking deposits. And if that means you have to switch banks for the loan, that's what you'll have to do - they will require it. You see, the more deposits a bank has, the more money it can loan out in an exponential manner. It's called the Fractional Reserve System, and in simple terms, the system is like a financial game of musical chairs (see *The Mystery of Banking* by Murray Rothbard for a detailed analysis)[10]. Banks are allowed to lend out substantially more money than they actually have. They only need to keep a fraction of their depositors' money on hand (that's the 'reserve') and can lend out the rest. This works because under normal circumstances not everyone needs all their money at once. But if everyone did want their money back at the same time, the bank wouldn't have enough to go around.

Consider this: If you have a $2.5M annual business, that means you are depositing roughly $200k per month of cash into somebody's bank. Of course, all of that money doesn't stay in your account because you have to pay payroll, accounts payable, and other expenses. It does mean, though, that you will carry a very healthy average depository balance in your account at all times.

---

[10] Rothbard, Murray N. *The Mystery of Banking*. 1st ed., Richardson & Snyder, 1983

This is what the bank will leverage to make a myriad of other loans; for example, car loans and credit cards. This diversifies their risk and nets them generally higher interest rates and with faster money turnover. All with **your money**.

Not to mention the fact that keeping your cash in the same bank that carries your mortgage debt is not a smart decision. It would be too easy for the bank to access your funds if they ever deemed it necessary - perhaps due to some loan covenant violation. And then, how do you make payroll?

Navigating the Fluid Expanse of Forces Affecting Your Options

The commercial financing landscape is ever-changing and influenced by numerous factors that can impact your options and ultimate success. To make the most informed decision, it's essential to understand these forces and how they shape your lending choices. Let's explore some of the key elements that contribute to the fluidity of financing:

1. **Economic Forces:** Fluctuating interest rates, economic growth, and market trends all play a significant role in determining the availability and terms of financing options. A strong economy might translate to more accessible loans with favorable terms, while economic downturns could lead to tighter lending

conditions. Staying informed about the current economic climate will help you better assess your options and make strategic decisions.

2. **Bank Regulators:** Regulatory bodies, such as the Federal Reserve, Office of the Comptroller of the Currency (OCC), and the Federal Deposit Insurance Corporation (FDIC), set guidelines and standards for lenders. These regulations can affect loan approval criteria, documentation requirements, and risk management practices, ultimately shaping the lending landscape. By understanding the regulatory environment, you'll be better equipped to navigate the complex world of commercial financing.

3. **Lender's Portfolio Desires and Requirements[11]:** Each lender has its own unique strategy, risk tolerance, and target market. Some may focus on specific industries, property types, or geographic areas, while others might prioritize loans with certain risk profiles or loan-to-value (LTV) ratios. This means that even if one lender turns you down, another might find your loan request appealing. Researching and identifying

---

[11] These change more often than the typical politician's *unswerving* commitments to garner votes.

lenders with compatible portfolio requirements will increase your chances of securing the right financing option.

4. **Industry and Space Type Trends:** Lenders are constantly monitoring market trends and adjusting their lending strategies accordingly. Certain industries or commercial space types may be more attractive to lenders at any given time, depending on factors such as demand, growth potential, and perceived risk. Being aware of these trends will allow you to better position your business and property for financing success.

5. **Governmental and Political Influences:** Changes in government policy, such as tax laws and regulations, can impact the lending environment. In addition, global economic events, such as recessions or trade disputes, can also influence lending conditions. Staying informed about these factors will help you better anticipate potential challenges and adapt your financing strategy accordingly.

Making An Informed Decision: The Importance of Professional Guidance in Finding Your Perfect Solution

As you can see, choosing the right financing option for your commercial property can be a complex and challenging process. With so many variables to consider and the fluid nature of the lending market, it's essential to have expert guidance to navigate this intricate landscape. A professional advisor with experience and knowledge can help you find the perfect "solution set" tailored to your unique situation and needs, ensuring that you make the best decision for your long-term success.

One of the aspects to consider is that not all lenders, particularly those offering Small Business Administration (SBA) loans, are created equally. Lenders have varying levels of SBA authority, with some having more autonomy and flexibility in approving loans than others. This can significantly impact the application process, the loan terms, and ultimately, the likelihood of securing financing.

An experienced advisor will be able to identify the most compatible lenders for your specific needs, as well as navigate the nuances of the lending process. They can help you understand the differences between SBA 7A, 504, and other loan types, ensuring you choose the option that best aligns with your goals and objectives. Moreover, a professional advisor can provide invaluable insights into the benefits and drawbacks of each option, helping you make informed decisions based on your unique circumstances.

By enlisting the support of a knowledgeable professional, you can avoid potential pitfalls and costly mistakes in the financing process. They will work tirelessly to ensure you secure the optimal financing solution for your business, maximizing your chances of success.

It's time to finish the story of my friend Nathan. We worked together and secured an amazing deal for him. He was able to purchase the $1.5M warehouse with a low, 10% down payment and a 25 year, fixed rate term for the entire life of his loan. And with essentially no prepayment penalty and no depository requirements. He was delighted that he could keep an extra $150,000 in his operating account, giving him a solid cash cushion for the business. And that he could actually secure a long-term, fixed rate loan in the commercial space. As I'm reminded quite often throughout my life, ignorance of smart, available options is *not* bliss.

In the next chapter, we will delve into the art of strategic and effective ways to present yourself to the right lender in order to maximize your chances of securing the funding you need. By understanding the best practices in packaging your loan application, you'll be better prepared to make a winning impression and secure the financing you need to propel your business to new heights.

Chapter 11

Pitch Perfect: Nail Your First Financial Impression

"The first impression is the truth, and all that follows is merely the excuse." - Robert Brault

Securing the funds for your dream project can feel like an insurmountable challenge. The path is fraught with potential pitfalls, and even the savviest entrepreneurs can stumble if they're not careful. After all, every new client and loan represents a risk to the lender, and there are countless ways your application could be declined. But fear not, intrepid entrepreneur! With the right knowledge, plan, and execution, you can rise above the obstacles and achieve success in securing the financing you need.

You see, lenders aren't simply heartless gatekeepers, barring the way to your business dreams. They are rational actors, weighing the risks and rewards of each potential loan. Their primary concern is ensuring that they'll receive their investment back, with interest. By understanding this fundamental dynamic and learning how to present your case in the most compelling light, you can dramatically increase your chances of approval.

The key to victory is recognizing that first impressions are everything. Lenders see countless applications and they're adept at quickly identifying red flags that could spell trouble down the road. Your goal, then, is to create a presentation that is both persuasive and meticulous, leaving no stone unturned in demonstrating your worthiness as a borrower. This chapter was written to give you the expertise and guidance to help you navigate these treacherous waters, avoiding common mistakes and ensuring that your application stands head and shoulders above the rest.

First Impressions Matter

It is routinely said that we don't judge a book by its cover, but that's really not true. The cover matters - a lot. In his widely popular and influential book, *Blink: The Power of Thinking Without Thinking*,[12] Malcolm Gladwell introduces the idea of "thin-slicing," which refers to our ability to gauge what's really important from a very narrow period of experience. It is the

---

[12] Gladwell, Malcolm. *Blink: The Power of Thinking Without Thinking*. Little, Brown and Company, 2005

ability of our subconscious mind to find patterns in situations and behavior based on very narrow slices of experience. That spontaneous decisions are often as good as—or even better than—carefully planned and considered ones.

And when you're trying to secure funding for your new building, first impressions are everything. Approaching a lender without a solid, well-prepared case is like showing up to an important meeting in sweatpants. It sends the wrong message and undermines your credibility. To maximize your chances of success, you must present your best case from the outset, showcasing your commitment, professionalism, and understanding of the lender's perspective.

In today's digital age, it's more important than ever to be forthcoming about any potential challenges or issues that could arise during the lending process. Lenders have access to vast amounts of information, and any skeletons lurking in your closet will almost certainly be discovered. By addressing any and all of these issues upfront, you'll demonstrate your transparency and proactive approach to problem-solving.

For example, let's say you failed to disclose a previous bankruptcy during the initial stages of your loan application. This might seem like a minor oversight at first, but as the process progresses, the lender will inevitably uncover this crucial piece of information. When they do, it could throw the entire project into jeopardy. Had you been upfront about the bankruptcy from the beginning, you could have worked together with the lender to address their concerns and develop a strategy for mitigating the associated risks.

Remember, no business or individual is perfect, and lenders understand this. They're looking for borrowers who are honest, accountable, and prepared to address potential challenges head-on. By being transparent about any issues and presenting a comprehensive plan to overcome them, you'll not only earn the lender's trust but also significantly increase your chances of securing the funding you need.

In short, the key to winning over lenders is to present your best case from the **start**. This means doing your homework, understanding the lender's concerns, and addressing any potential issues proactively. When you do this, you'll stand head and shoulders above most other loan applicants that they are considering and position yourself for success.

Navigating the Landmines and Pitfalls

Being aware of some of the most common obstacles and knowing how to navigate them is imperative to your success. In this section, we'll delve into some common landmines and provide valuable insights on how to sidestep them:

1. **Not having your spouse on board:** In many cases, the support and cooperation of your

spouse is essential to securing financing. Ensure that you're both aligned with the goals and objectives of your business venture before approaching lenders.

2. **Covenants and how to avoid them:** Loan covenants can impose stringent conditions on your business operations, limiting your flexibility and control (see *Corporate Credit: A CFO's Guide to Bank Debt and Loan Agreements* by Susan Alker for a detailed explanation).[13] To minimize their impact, negotiate with lenders to secure favorable terms and maintain open lines of communication throughout the lending process.

3. **Using your home as collateral and how to avoid it:** Pledging your home as collateral can put your personal assets at risk. Investigate alternative forms of collateral or explore financing options that don't require this level of personal commitment.

4. **Lenders requiring your deposits and why that's a bad idea:** Some lenders may request that you move a substantial amount of your business

---

[13] Alker, Susan. *Corporate Credit: A CFO's Guide to Bank Debt and Loan Agreements*. Independent, 2020

deposits to their institution as a condition of the loan. This can limit your financial flexibility and create conflicts of interest. Explore alternative options and negotiate terms that safeguard your financial independence.

5. **Moving too fast – patience is a requirement:** Rushing into a commercial loan can lead to poor decision-making and suboptimal outcomes. Take the time to research, compare, and negotiate the best financing options for your specific needs.

6. **Little to no post-closing cash reserves:** Maintaining a healthy cash reserve after closing the loan is essential for weathering unexpected challenges and ensuring the ongoing success of your business. Plan your finances accordingly and prioritize building a cash cushion.

7. **Not working with a professional realtor:** Partnering with an experienced commercial real estate agent can help you find the ideal property, negotiate favorable terms, and navigate the complexities of the commercial property market. Don't underestimate the value of professional expertise in this critical area.

By understanding and addressing these common pitfalls and challenges, you'll be better equipped to secure the financing you need and set the stage for a successful and prosperous venture. Remember, knowledge is power, and being well-informed about potential obstacles will put you in a strong position to navigate the process successfully.

Unlocking Success with a Trusted Advocate: The Advantages of Professional Guidance in Securing Your Loan

> *"Great things in business are never done by one person; they're done by a team of people." - Steve Jobs*

Alright, now, let's move on to the third key point. You see, sometimes it's a brilliant idea to get someone in your corner when you're dealing with lenders. It's kind of like enlisting a super-smart, savvy and experienced friend who knows the ins and outs of the game. Let's face it, none of us know everything. This is especially true when dealing with lenders and all the complicated financial jargon. It's like trying to navigate through a new city without a map or GPS.

So what does it mean to have someone represent you to the lender? Well, it's like having a skilled negotiator on your side, a champion who speaks the lender's language and knows how to present your case in the best light. This expert can read the room, anticipate what the lender might ask, and help you prepare the answers.

Why is that a good idea? Well, it's like having a coach or mentor in any field. The guidance of someone with experience and expertise can significantly improve your chances of getting the best deal. It's not just about getting approved for the loan; it's about securing the best terms possible.

Now, you may be wondering, what's the cost of getting this helping hand? I hear you. But think about it, what's the cost of not having this support? What's the cost of potentially missing out on the best deal or, worse, not getting approved at all because you didn't understand something? That's a price too steep to pay.

How do you know where to find someone like this? How do you find an impartial, knowledgeable ally who's got your back, not the lender's? Someone who understands the market in depth and can guide you through this complex process?

This is where a good commercial loan broker comes into the mix. **A successful, reputable broker will have a dedicated team representing you to a host of the right lenders - not representing the lender to you.** They will have deep market knowledge, coupled with strong business experience giving them insights that they will leverage for your benefit, resulting in you getting the best possible deal.

Effective brokers get paid when they secure the funding for you and help you win, so they have a vested interest in your success. So consider letting a great commercial loan broker be your champion, your coach, and together you can navigate the complex world of commercial real estate financing in the most efficient, effective manner possible.

In the next chapter, we'll explore the closing process, also known as loan delivery. You've been approved, but what comes next?

Chapter 12

Post–Approval:
The Next Adventure Awaits

"The finish line is just the beginning of a whole new race." – Unknown

Securing approval for your loan is a significant milestone in your entrepreneurial journey, but the process is far from over. As you transition from approval to closing, it's important to maintain the same level of focus, determination, and attention to detail that brought you this far. In this chapter, we will guide you through the stages of the loan delivery process, ensuring you are well-prepared for each step and can avoid any remaining obstacles with confidence.

We will explore the intricacies of the post-approval world, discussing the expectations you should have, the closing process, and the overall timeline you need to be aware of. By the end of this chapter, you will be well-equipped to handle the challenges that lie ahead, ensuring a seamless transition from loan approval to property ownership.

Expectations and Loan Commitment

Now that your loan has been approved, you will receive a **loan commitment** from the lender. This document outlines the final terms and conditions of your loan, including interest rates, repayment schedules, and any additional requirements.

It's essential to carefully review and understand your loan commitment, as it serves as the foundation for your loan agreement. It's possible that some of the terms may have changed from the initial term sheet that you received. This can be caused by a number of factors, including market changes, underwriting findings, and even credit issues. Now that you have the commitment letter in hand, the terms of your loan have been approved and are set.

Navigating the Closing Process

Bear in mind that closing a commercial loan is a different process from closing a residential mortgage. The timeline can be longer, and there may be additional requirements to fulfill. Generally, the entire closing process can take several weeks to a month, depending on the complexity of the transaction and the lender's requirements.

One critical aspect of the closing process is the completion and approval of third-party reports, such as title, survey, and environmental studies. These reports play a vital role in protecting both you and the lender by ensuring that the property is free of any encumbrances, zoning issues, or environmental hazards that could jeopardize your investment. Many lenders order and review these reports during the underwriting phase and ensure that all is in order before actually issuing a loan commitment, but some will wait until the very end of the process.

Another essential step is verifying your closing funds, which must be both sourced and seasoned. Lenders will scrutinize your recent 60-90 days of banking history, ensuring that the funds you're using for the purchase have been in your account for a specified period and originate from legitimate sources.

Throughout the closing process, you may encounter paperwork and documentation that needs to be corrected or signed, which is very normal, but can be frustrating. This is where having a team of trusted professionals, such as a broker, attorney, accountant, and real estate agent, can prove invaluable. They can help you navigate the complexities of the closing process and ensure that everything is in order before you proceed to the final stage.

Taking a Step Back: Understanding the Overall Timeline

The entire journey of purchasing a commercial property can be divided into five phases:

Phase I - Contemplating the Big Move: This initial phase is all about introspection and research. Evaluate your current business needs, growth potential, and the advantages of owning a commercial property. Consult with industry experts and gather essential information to make an informed decision.

Phase II - Pre-approval and Securing Term Sheets: Before jumping into the property search, seek pre-approval from potential lenders to understand your borrowing capacity. This phase involves gathering documentation, assessing your financial position, and obtaining term sheets that outline the proposed loan structure and terms.

Phase III - Finding and Making an Offer on a Space: With a clear understanding of your financial capabilities, partner with a commercial real estate agent to search for the perfect property. Once you've identified the ideal space, negotiate the purchase terms, and make a formal offer.

Phase IV - Loan Underwriting: After your offer is accepted, the lender will thoroughly evaluate your financial standing, the property's condition, and market factors. This phase may involve appraisals, environmental studies, and title searches to ensure the property is a sound investment.

Phase V - Closing: Upon receiving the loan commitment, you'll enter the final stage of the process: closing. This phase requires attention to detail, as you'll need to verify closing funds, sign paperwork, and complete any outstanding requirements.

Understanding the timeline of the commercial property acquisition journey helps you set realistic expectations for yourself and your team. As we move on to the next chapter, we will explore strategies and tips for managing this journey without derailing your daily business commitments. With the right approach and guidance, you can successfully secure the perfect commercial property to elevate your business to new heights.

Chapter 13

Into Action: Strategies to Set the Stage

"Someday is not a day of the week." - Janet Dailey

Embarking on the journey to acquire the building to house your business is a significant decision, one that can potentially transform your company's future. The process, however, can be complex and time-consuming, especially for those who are new to commercial real estate. As you forge ahead, you need to understand the various approaches available for successfully navigating the pathway.

In this chapter, we'll explore three primary strategies for tackling the acquisition process. Each approach comes with its own set of advantages and challenges, and it's essential to weigh your options carefully before deciding on the path that best aligns with your needs, resources, and business goals.

We'll examine the do-it-yourself (DIY) approach, which requires substantial investment in time and effort but allows for more direct control over the process. We'll also discuss the possibility of enlisting a staff member, such as your CFO, who can bring professional expertise to the table but may lack specialized market knowledge. Lastly, we'll delve into the benefits of engaging a dedicated professional or team with extensive expertise in the financial marketplace to ensure you secure the best possible terms and conditions for your investment.

Consider the unique aspects of your business and how each approach could impact your ability to achieve your long-term objectives. By making an informed decision, you'll be better equipped to navigate the complexities of the commercial real estate market and unlock the full potential of property ownership for your business.

The DIY Option: Navigating the Commercial Financing Landscape on Your Own

While the DIY approach may seem appealing at first, it's essential to understand the potential drawbacks and hidden costs associated with taking on the responsibility of securing a commercial property for your business.

First and foremost, the time investment required for this process cannot be understated. Commercial property acquisition involves a myriad of tasks, such as preparing financials, developing a compelling pitch for lenders, seeking out potential financing options, and evaluating the pros and cons of each offer. Balancing these demands with the day-to-day operations of your business can be incredibly challenging, potentially leading to increased stress and a negative impact on your overall productivity.

Furthermore, the opportunity cost of dedicating your time and energy to the property search and financing process must be considered. The time spent navigating the complexities of commercial real estate could be better invested in growing your business, nurturing client relationships, or developing new products or services. In essence, every hour you spend on this project is an hour taken away from other valuable pursuits that directly contribute to the success of your company.

In addition to the time commitment, the DIY approach also exposes you to potential pitfalls due to a lack of expertise and experience in the commercial property market. For instance, you may not be aware of the full range of financing options available or have the necessary connections to secure the best possible terms. This limited perspective could result in missed opportunities or settling for suboptimal financing arrangements that negatively impact your bottom line.

Moreover, the stress of managing the acquisition process on your own can take an emotional toll. As the sole decision-maker, the pressure to secure the right property and financing can be overwhelming, leading to potential frustration or burnout. This emotional strain can also cloud your judgment, making it more challenging to assess the merits of each financing option objectively.

It's also essential to consider the hidden costs and potential drawbacks of this approach. The time, effort, and emotional investment required to successfully navigate the process can be substantial, and the opportunity cost of diverting your attention from other vital aspects of your business should not be overlooked. Before deciding to go it alone, carefully weigh the benefits against the potential costs and consider whether this approach truly aligns with your long-term business goals.

Delegation: Balancing Expertise and Limited Resources

Another approach to the problem is to delegate some or all of the process to a team member so you can continue to focus on your core business-building activities. This can allow you to stay mission-focused and still achieve the goal of acquiring the property.

While it might seem like a logical solution to delegate the process to a staff member such as your CFO, it's vital to recognize the potential limitations and risks associated with this approach.

One primary concern is the bandwidth and workload of your existing staff. Taking on the additional responsibilities of property acquisition and financing can be a daunting task, requiring a significant amount of time and focus. This additional workload may lead to decreased productivity in their core job functions, ultimately impacting the overall performance of your business. In the worst-case scenario, the added stress may lead to employee burnout, turnover, or a negative impact on team morale.

Moreover, while your CFO or other staff member may possess financial acumen, they may not have the specialized knowledge, experience, or industry connections needed to navigate the intricacies of the market effectively. This lack of specific expertise could result in an incomplete or superficial understanding of the available properties or financing options, leading to less favorable deals or even missed opportunities.

Additionally, an internal team member may not be as committed to securing the best possible deal for your business as an external expert. They may settle for a solution that is *good enough* rather than investing the time and effort required to explore all potential avenues. Furthermore, they may not have the same level of motivation or drive to negotiate the *most favorable* terms for your business.

Another risk associated with relying on your staff for your acquisition is the potential for tunnel vision or confirmation bias (see *Thinking, Fast and Slow* by Daniel Kehneman for an in-depth analysis).[14] An internal team member may approach the process with preconceived notions or beliefs about what financing options are best for your business, potentially leading to a narrow perspective that overlooks more advantageous opportunities.

Lastly, delegating the acquisition process to an existing staff member can also create a potential conflict of interest. Your employee may feel compelled to make decisions that protect their own job security or standing within the company, rather than prioritizing the best interests of your business as a whole.

Balancing the additional workload, lack of specialized expertise, commitment to finding the best deals, and the possibility of conflicts of interest are all critical factors to consider before entrusting this considerable task to your staff.

---

[14] Kahneman, Daniel. *Thinking, Fast and Slow*. 1st ed., Farrar, Straus and Giroux, 2011

The Benefits of Engaging a Professional Team: Embracing the "Who Not How" Philosophy

> *"Do what you do best and outsource the rest." - Peter Drucker*

The *Who Not How*[15] philosophy, largely introduced by leadership coach and author Dan Sullivan and codified in his book of the same name, emphasizes the importance and effectiveness of finding the right people and enlisting their help to achieve your goals. He argues that you can be much more effective by clearly identifying a desired outcome and seeking the best people to get it done, rather than by focusing your time trying to understand the methodology of actual implementation. By adopting this approach, you can tap into the expertise and skills of professionals who specialize in property acquisition and financing, significantly increasing your chances of success.

Choosing to work with a professional team brings numerous benefits. The right team will consist of, at a minimum, a commercial real estate agent and a commercial

---

[15] Sullivan, Dan, and Benjamin Hardy. *Who Not How: The Formula to Achieve Bigger Goals Through Accelerating Teamwork*. 1st ed., Hay House, Inc., 2020

loan broker. This could also extend out to include a great real estate attorney and CPA.

Consider the commercial loan broker…First and foremost, they have extensive knowledge and experience in the field, providing access to a national marketplace of financing options. That expertise enables them to identify and secure the best sources for getting you the right funding for your specific needs, ensuring you receive the most favorable terms and conditions available.

Furthermore, they represent your interests throughout the process, acting as your advocate, rather than representing a particular lending source. This impartiality allows them to focus on finding the most suitable solutions for your business, without any hidden agendas or biases.

Having third-party emotional detachment from the transaction allows your advocate to maintain objectivity, enabling them to make clear-headed decisions on your behalf. This impartiality is imperative when navigating the complex landscape of commercial financing, as it helps prevent clouded judgment or irrational decisions driven by personal attachment.

Another significant advantage of working with a professional team is their ability to help you avoid potential pitfalls and roadblocks during the process. They can guide you through the various stages, offering valuable insights and advice to help you sidestep potential issues that could derail your project, saving you time and frustration.

Ultimately, engaging a professional team empowers you to concentrate on what you do best – running and growing your business – while they handle the complex and time-consuming task of securing the ideal commercial property financing for your needs.

As we move into the next chapter, we'll explore some of the additional benefits of owning and how it can contribute to your long-term success.

Chapter 14

More Than Meets the Eye: Ownership's Hidden Perks

"Just when you think there is nothing left, dig deeper. There is more strength, more ideas, more hope. But wait... there's more!" - Billy Blanks

As we close our journey together, we will consider some often-overlooked benefits of owning your commercial space. As you've seen throughout this book, owning your property provides numerous advantages for your business, from financial gains to increased stability. But that's just part of the story!

You'll discover the transformative effects that property ownership can have on your relationships with customers, employees, and the community at large. So, let's dive into these hidden gems, and uncover the true value that lies beneath the surface.

The Case for Permanence and Community Impact

Jane is a driven entrepreneur who owns a thriving catering service in the Tampa, Florida area. She is known for her exceptional menus and attention to detail. However, she worked from a rented commercial kitchen and was constantly dealing with the limitations of her lease. The day she decided to own her kitchen space, her journey to lasting community impact truly began.

Owning your commercial space expands beyond just financial opportunity. It's a significant move that cements your presence in the local community and sends a clear message of commitment to your customers and employees.

When Jane purchased her building, she wasn't just buying property; she was investing in the community. As a property owner, her relationships with her customers deepened. They saw her business not just as a service but as a community asset, an establishment committed to the area's future. This trust transformed into customer loyalty, providing stability, especially during tough economic times.

And owning her space offered Jane a platform to give back to her community. As one example, her kitchen became more than a commercial space; it became a community center that hosted cooking classes, food drives, and other local events. It enabled Jane to build long-term relationships within the local community. Her establishment became a cornerstone, supporting community events and initiatives, making her business a cherished local hub.

Owning the space also significantly affected Jane's team who saw their workplace as more than a rented space—it was their home, a symbol of the stability and success of their employer. This pride reflected in their work, enhancing their dedication and boosting the overall productivity of Jane's catering service. Her employees also saw her commitment to the business's longevity and felt more secure in their jobs. This trust translated into a vibrant company culture and increased productivity, directly impacting the success of her catering business.

In addition, there is also a profound sense of pride that comes with ownership. When Jane now walks into her own kitchen, she isn't just entering a building; she is stepping into a testament to her hard work and success. This sense of achievement infuses every decision she makes, fostering confident leadership that positively impacts her business's trajectory.

Owning commercial property, therefore, isn't merely about owning a building; it's about fostering community ties, cementing your commitment to your business, and creating a lasting legacy that transcends financial gains. It's a journey towards creating an impact and empowering your business to become an integral part of your community's story.

Leverage And Additional Real Estate Investing Opportunities

As an astute business owner, you understand the importance of diversifying your investments and building long-term wealth. One of the often-overlooked benefits of owning your commercial space is the potential to leverage that real estate into other investment opportunities. By acquiring your own commercial property, you've already taken the first step towards creating a thriving real estate portfolio.

In *Rich Dad, Poor Dad,*[16] Robert Kiyosaki emphasizes the power of real estate as a tool for building wealth and achieving financial independence. As a commercial property owner, you are uniquely positioned to capitalize on this strategy by exploring additional real estate investment opportunities. These could include office buildings, multifamily properties, vacation rentals, or even industrial spaces.

The skills, experience and equity you will gain from acquiring your own commercial space can be invaluable in navigating the world of real estate investing. You'll be better equipped to recognize lucrative opportunities and manage the unique challenges associated with each type of property. This knowledge, combined with the financial leverage provided by your existing real estate holdings, can help you grow your portfolio and generate passive income streams.

---

[16] Kiyosaki, Robert T. *Rich Dad Poor Dad.* Warner Books Ed, 2000

As your business expands, you may also consider purchasing additional commercial spaces to house new locations or branches of your operation. This strategy can further solidify your presence in the market, enhancing the stability and long-term success of your enterprise.

Why Not Multiply Your Presence and Your Wealth?

Allow me to share the remarkable journey of Dr. Alan, a distinguished dentist with an entrepreneurial spirit. When Alan opened his first dental practice, he made a strategic decision that set him apart from most dentists — he quickly bought the building his practice was located in.

Alan knew that he wanted to provide unparalleled service to his patients, but he also had a vision for expansion. His dream wasn't confined to one dental practice; he envisioned a network of practices across the region, all marked by the same commitment to quality care and housed in buildings he owned.

After the success of his first dental practice, within two years, Alan saw an opportunity for expansion. A prime commercial property in a neighboring town caught his eye. He took the leap, bought the building, and launched his second location. Patients in the area quickly came to trust Alan and his team, appreciating their consistent, quality service.

Three years later, Alan saw potential for growth in another nearby town. Relying on his established strategy, he purchased another commercial building, transforming it into his third dental practice. His reputation as a reliable dentist offering superior service preceded him, making this expansion successful as well.

Continuing his pattern of strategic expansion, the good dentist added two more practices to his portfolio over the next several years, each in different towns and each in buildings that he owned. His patient base quickly grew, as did his team. He was able to recruit top talent who were drawn to the stability of his expanding operation.

By year ten, he owned five successful dental practices, each housed in its own building. His strategic decision to purchase rather than lease the properties his practices were located in gave him control and stability. It also allowed him to leverage the equity in those properties for future expansions, effectively fueling his growth.

Alan's journey showcases the potential of strategic real estate investment as part of business expansion. He didn't just grow his dental practice; he built a robust enterprise, marked by stability and longevity. His strategy solidified his presence across the region, providing a platform for sustained success.

You Can Diversify and Strengthen Your Future

By diversifying your real estate holdings, you can protect yourself from economic fluctuations and market changes, ensuring that your wealth continues to grow even during challenging times. One of the keys to financial freedom lies in generating multiple streams of income, and investing in various types of real estate can help you achieve this goal.

Another visionary entrepreneur, Jennifer, is an owner of a successful digital marketing agency in Nashville, TN, who began her journey as a business owner in a small rented office space. Within a few years, her agency had grown significantly, and it became evident that a larger office space was needed.

Instead of leasing a bigger space, Jennifer decided to buy a two-story commercial building in a thriving business district. This move not only provided her company with the much-needed room to grow, but it also accelerated Jennifer's path towards financial independence.

Once her agency was settled in the new building, Jennifer had an ingenious idea. She noticed that the second floor of her building had more space than her business needed, so she decided to convert it into a coworking space. This move generated a steady rental income, and more importantly, it introduced her to the lucrative world of real estate investing.

Motivated by the success of her coworking space, Jennifer decided to diversify her investment portfolio. After a couple of years, she purchased a small apartment building, using the equity she had built in her commercial property. She refurbished the units and began to rent them out, creating yet another stream of passive income.

The success of her initial real estate investments spurred Jennifer to explore more opportunities. Over the last decade, she has continued to leverage the growing equity in her commercial building to finance additional investments. She ventured into different types of real estate, from multi-family properties to storage units and even a small strip mall.

These investments were far from Jennifer's primary business of digital marketing, yet they played a significant role in her financial journey. Over time, the passive income generated by her real estate portfolio matched, and eventually exceeded, the income from her digital marketing agency. Jennifer's strategic investment in her commercial space had evolved into a wealth-building engine, propelling her towards financial independence.

Jennifer's story is a prime example of how owning commercial space can serve as a stepping stone towards broader real estate investment opportunities. By leveraging the equity in her agency's building, Jennifer could diversify her portfolio, generate passive income, and attain financial independence, all while running a successful digital marketing agency.

Owning your commercial space not only provides immediate benefits to your business but also opens the door to a wealth of additional real estate investment opportunities. By capitalizing on these prospects, you can create a thriving, diverse portfolio that fuels your financial independence and long-term success.

Wrapping Up

Here we are, standing on the threshold of wrapping up our journey together. Throughout this ride, we've had some real talk about the ins and outs of owning your own commercial space. We've traversed the landscape of benefits, opportunities, and the profound impact it can have on your business' success. But, it's not quite over yet!

As we transition into the final chapter of our odyssey, we're going to pull together the lessons learned, the revelations uncovered, and the *ah-ha* moments we've shared. We'll be tying it all up neatly, but we're also going to add a finishing touch.

This last part isn't just about relishing our victories and planning for that prosperous future; it's about staring down the potential pitfalls to avoid too. We're going to address the stumbling blocks, the roadblocks, the wrenches that could get tossed in our well-intentioned plans. And these are not external factors, my friend. We're talking about self-sabotage—those subtle ways we can hold ourselves back without even realizing it.

But don't worry, knowledge is power. Recognizing these obstacles is the first step towards avoiding them, towards moving forward with the courage, the conviction, and the clarity needed to claim your envisioned future.

Chapter 15

Journey's End: Igniting Your Vision

"Two roads diverged in a wood, and I— I took the one less traveled by, And that has made all the difference." - Robert Frost

Have you ever tried to imagine the future? That bright, sparkling horizon just beyond our reach? As we close out this journey we've taken together, let's immerse ourselves in that future—the one you've been striving for, that ideal tomorrow when you're not just running your business, but you're doing it from the command center of your very own commercial space. It's a vision worth marinating in, don't you think?

Imagine the crack of dawn on an ordinary business day. The world is still half-asleep as you draw open the curtains of your bedroom window, but your pulse quickens with anticipation. You get ready and drive to your building, the sweet aroma of fresh morning air permeating through the car window, whispering promises of a new beginning, a new day, and endless possibilities.

Now picture the moment you pull up to your commercial space. Your space. It stands there, sturdy and grand, a testament to your perseverance and ambition. The morning sun reflects off the glass facade, and as you look up, you see more than just a building. You see your hard work and dedication made tangible, a testament to your dreams materialized, and it's like seeing the sun rise on a world of opportunities that's now within your grasp.

Stepping out of your car, you can hear the city waking up around you, the distant hum of traffic, the soft chime of your building's entrance as you glide through the door. The echo in the vast lobby rings with the sound of your footsteps, each step a symbol of the journey you've taken, the battles you've fought, and the victories you've won.

As you walk into your office, you can feel the cool, smooth surface of your desk under your fingertips. The robust aroma of freshly brewed coffee wafts from the office kitchen, grounding you in the present moment—the tangible reality of your accomplishments.

And the day hasn't even started yet.

Your employees start to filter in, and their respectful nods and smiles are a reflection of your winning culture, and in their eyes, you see the same fire, the same commitment you bring to your work every day. As the day unfolds, the hum of productivity fills your space, and it's a sound more satisfying than any symphony.

Can you feel the sense of *fulfillment*? This feeling is more than just owning a building. It's a daily reminder that you've etched your mark in the world, that you've built something lasting. It's not just a financial investment—it's an investment in your future, in your dream.

And as the day winds down, you take a moment to reflect, to appreciate the monument to success that you've created. Your business is more than just a revenue stream— it's a part of you, a part of your identity, and you can see that identity reflected back at you every time you look at your very own commercial space.

Remember, this isn't a dream. This is the reality that awaits you when you decide to own your space. It's a reality within your grasp, one that is filled with pride, accomplishment, and a sense of profound satisfaction that permeates every aspect of your life.

Be Careful Not to Derail Your Dream

As you consider this dream, let's also revisit some of the snags that can derail your progress if you're not careful. You must take the necessary steps to avoid them as you pursue the goal of being the owner:

1. **Seeking advice from those who have failed in business or never owned a business:** Surround yourself with knowledgeable, experienced individuals who can provide valuable insights and guidance. They've walked the path you're on and can help you navigate the challenges ahead.

2. **Not securing your spouse's support from the beginning:** Owning a commercial space is a significant decision that will impact your family's future. Ensure that your spouse is on board and aligned with your goals to avoid unnecessary conflict and misaligned expectations.

3. **Making major purchases during the process:** Keep your financial standing stable during this critical time. Unnecessary purchases can negatively impact your loan approval and ultimately hinder your ability to buy the commercial space you desire.

4. **Concealing any personal or financial "skeletons":** Be upfront and honest about any potential issues that could surface later and undermine your credibility.

5. **Failing to respond promptly to requests for information:** Communication is key in any successful endeavor, and this is no exception.

Delays and missed opportunities can result from a lack of responsiveness, so be proactive in providing the necessary information and documentation.

6. **Neglecting to engage a professional commercial realtor:** Finding and negotiating the best possible deal for your commercial space requires the expertise of a seasoned professional. Don't leave this important aspect of the process to chance.

7. **Not putting your best foot forward from the beginning:** First impressions are lasting with lenders. Be thoroughly prepared before you engage them in your financing journey. Missing or incomplete information can result in delays, frustration, and lenders don't like to "work" to understand or discern your particular case. It's easier for them to just say no.

8. **Procrastination and waiting for the perfect time:** Remember, opportunities come and go. Embrace the concept of seeking a 'who' rather than a 'how' to ensure your success. Taking action today can be the difference between realizing your dream and watching it slip through your fingers.

As you stand on the precipice of this exciting new chapter in your entrepreneurial journey, envision the incredible future that lies ahead. Picture the thriving business you'll expand within the walls of your very own space. Imagine the impact you'll have on your employees, your customers, and your community as you demonstrate your unwavering commitment to their success and well-being.

The Time is Now, and The Decision is Yours Alone

I want to leave you with a story that has resonated with me over the years as I've considered my own life and business journey[17].

There was once a wise old man who was known throughout the town for his wisdom and intelligence. A young boy, intrigued and somewhat skeptical of the old man's reputation, decided to trick him in order to prove he wasn't as smart as everyone believed.

The boy caught a small sparrow, cupping it in his hands and approached the old man. His plan was to ask the old man if the bird was dead or alive. If the old man said the bird was dead, the boy would open his hands and

---

[17] I'm not exactly sure where I first heard this anecdote, or where it originated. Perhaps it was from my crusty old 8th grade gym teacher Mr. Anderson trying to motivate me to join the wrestling team?

let the bird fly away. If the old man said the bird was alive, the boy would crush the bird in his hands, proving the old man wrong.

He approached the wise man with the bird hidden in his hands and asked, "Old man, is the bird in my hands alive or dead?" The old man looked at the boy, pondered for a moment, and then replied, "The answer, my boy, is in your hands."

And you are also holding your future in your hands. But to achieve this dream, you must take action. It's time to step out of your comfort zone and embrace the challenge of owning your commercial space. Don't let fear or indecision hold you back from seizing this opportunity. Your dream is within reach, and me and my team are here to help you make it a reality.

We want to be your partner in this journey, guiding you through the process and leveraging our expertise and experience to ensure your success. Our team is dedicated to understanding your unique needs, goals, and aspirations, and we are committed to helping you make the best possible decisions for the future of your business.

But it all begins with a single, big step: reaching out to us for an *Ownership Strategy Session* call. This initial discussion is an opportunity for us to learn more about your business, your vision, and your challenges. Together, we'll explore the various options available to you and help you determine if this opportunity makes sense for you or not.

So, take a moment to reflect on everything we've discussed throughout this book. Consider the powerful benefits of owning your commercial space, the perils to avoid, and the invaluable guidance and expertise that our team can provide. Then, take a deep breath and embrace the challenge that lies ahead. Your dream is within reach, and the journey to achieve it starts now.

The time has come for you to seize this opportunity and create the thriving, successful future you've always envisioned for your business. Don't let this moment pass you by. Contact us today and take the first step towards making your dream a reality.

I sincerely hope that the insights and guidance I've provided in our journey together have inspired you to take the bold leap into this exciting new chapter in your life as a business owner. Remember, the path to success is rarely easy or straightforward, but with determination, perseverance, and the right team by your side, there's no limit to what you can achieve.

Take the Next Step: Schedule a 20 Minute Ownership Strategy Session

Dive deeper into the wealth-building strategies from 'Unlease Your Business.' Join me for an *Ownership Strategy Session* call and let's find out if it makes sense for you to transition from renter to owner. In this conversation, we'll explore your potential to turn rent payments into valuable equity. Ready to unlock your business potential? Let's start strategizing!

www.OwnYourBuildingNow.com/Schedule

OR

Unlock Your Bonus Content NOW!

Reading 'Un-lease Your Business' is already a big step towards securing your future, but why stop there?

Accelerate your journey by accessing a suite of exclusive FREE resources, designed to deepen your understanding and fast-track your success.

1. *The Ultimate Guide to Evaluating a Property:* Get your hands on our straightforward, step-by-step checklist to aid you in making an informed decision when eyeing that potential property. Understand the nuances of property evaluation, making it a smooth ride for you.

2. *Expert Insights: A Multi-Part Video Course:* Gain critical insights from seasoned professionals who've walked the path you're about to tread. It's like having a panel of top-notch mentors right at your fingertips, helping you navigate your way to real estate wealth.

3. *Profitable Transitions: Real-World Case Studies of Entrepreneurs Turning Rent into Equity:* Hear directly from those who've done it. Their trials, tribulations, and triumphs - unfiltered, insightful, and most importantly, applicable to your own journey.

Visit the link or scan the QR code to access these powerful tools now. Remember, the road to business freedom and wealth creation begins with the first step.

Let these resources be your compass, guiding you towards a future of property ownership and financial independence. It's time to 'Unlease Your Business' and write your own success story!"

www.OwnYourBuildingNow.com/Resources

OR

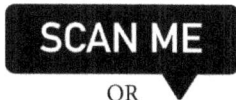

Bibliography

Kiyosaki, Robert T. *Rich Dad Poor Dad*. Warner Books Ed, 2000

Womack, James P., Daniel T. Jones, and Daniel Roos. *The Machine That Changed the World*. Rawson Associates, 1990

United States, Internal Revenue Service. *How To Depreciate Property*. Publication 946, 2022. https://www.irs.gov/publications/p946

United States, Internal Revenue Service. *Cost Segregation Audit Technique Guide*. 2022

Hahn, Amanda, and Matthew Macfarland. *The Book on Tax Strategies for the Savvy Real Estate Investor: Powerful techniques anyone can use to deduct more, invest smarter, and pay far less to the IRS!* BiggerPockets; First Edition. 2016

U.S. Small Business Administration. "SOP 10 7: Standard Operating Procedure for Small Business Loans." August 1, 2023. U.S. Small Business Administration, https://www.sba.gov/document/sop-50-10-lender-development-company-loan-programs

Rothbard, Murray N. *The Mystery of Banking*. 1st ed., Richardson & Snyder, 1983

Gladwell, Malcolm. *Blink: The Power of Thinking Without Thinking*. Little, Brown and Company, 2005

Alker, Susan. *Corporate Credit: A CFO's Guide to Bank Debt and Loan Agreements*. Independent, 2020

Kahneman, Daniel. *Thinking, Fast and Slow*. 1st ed., Farrar, Straus and Giroux, 2011

Sullivan, Dan, and Benjamin Hardy. *Who Not How: The Formula to Achieve Bigger Goals Through Accelerating Teamwork*. 1st ed., Hay House, Inc., 2020

Kiyosaki, Robert T. *Rich Dad Poor Dad*. Warner Books Ed, 2000

About the Author

Paul Neal is the founder, CEO and Principal Funding Strategist at Vantage Point Commercial Capital, LLC, a firm that focuses on helping entrepreneurs, businesses, and real estate investors win by funding their growth and dreams in nontraditional ways.

Paul's unique perspective has been honed over 30 years as an entrepreneur, financial strategist, professional speaker, and executive coach. He took the road less traveled choosing to leave engineering right out of college to become a serial entrepreneur.

Since 1998, he and his team have helped scores of clients attain the funding they needed to advance their businesses and dreams. His driving belief is that when entrepreneurs build successful, growing, sustainable businesses that increase their wealth, everyone wins. They win. Their families win. Their employees win. Their community wins. They are the backbone of this country, and they have the resources and influence to drive true, grass roots, positive societal change.

When not funding some new venture, Paul enjoys the significant relationships in his life: starting with a deep commitment to his Christian faith, his beautiful wife Becky of many years, and with his inspiring, talented daughter Sarah, a future fighter jet pilot. He's also an avid runner, having completed numerous marathons and half-marathons, and loves to take the family skiing and diving each year.

Connect with Paul:

Visit his website: https://paulneal.net
LinkedIn: https://www.linkedin.com/in/paul-neal-47b8478
Vantage Point Commercial Capital: https://vpc.capital
Check out his podcast: *The Entrepreneurial Agent*
Check out on YouTube: *@theEntrepreneurialAgent*

www.ingramcontent.com/pod-product-compliance
Lightning Source LLC
Chambersburg PA
CBHW060606200326
41521CB00007B/680